Pentatonic
KHANCEPTS

BY STEVE KHAN

D1737390

WARNER BROS. PUBLICATIONS
Warner Music Group
An AOL Time Warner Company
USA: 15800 NW 48th Avenue, Miami, FL 33014

IMP
INTERNATIONAL MUSIC PUBLICATIONS LIMITED
ENGLAND: GRIFFIN HOUSE,
161 HAMMERSMITH ROAD, LONDON W6 8BS

INTRODUCTION

This book has been in the works for many years. It was always my intention that it would serve as the linear adjunct to **CONTEMPORARY CHORD KHANCEPTS** and that these two books would then be able to function beautifully together. Like the aforementioned book, **PENTATONIC KHANCEPTS** shares with you a particular theoretical philosophy that is designed to give variety and flow to your improvisations. There is certainly nothing new about pentatonic improvising. However, perhaps it has just never been presented in quite this form and this manner. One early chapter in the book is dedicated to making certain that you clearly understand the distinction between what makes a pentatonic line different from a jazz line. Once that has been accomplished, the focus of the book narrows.

The materials are organized in a manner that shows you how to employ them quickly and with results you can hear immediately. In presenting the materials for this book, I've tried to keep things as simple as possible and to make certain that the terminology and language are consistent with my chordal publication. As with **CHORD KHANCEPTS,** my hope is that the sophistication of the ideas will appeal to players in all genres: not being "over the head" of those who might not be interested in the specifics of music theory and not seeming to "talk down" to those who might have already attained a high level of sophistication where music theory is concerned. Since the publication of **CHORD KHANCEPTS,** I have received many encouraging letters from those who have used the book and gained from it. I can only hope that the successful communication of ideas will be much the same for this book .

I believe there are aspects to the understanding of music and music theory that involve no **"magic."** I think that, at one time or another, all of us would have believed that everything we heard and saw in music was born of **"magic."** However, the further we take our individual studies, we find that there is a very mathematical logic to much of it. The "magic" element lies in the **interaction** of the people making the music. But, in almost all cases, there are reasons why music sounds good, and often those reasons are born of sound theory.

In this book I have tried to organize those theories that I very much want to share with you to appear in simple charts and tables so you can access the information quickly and with great accuracy. The theories, like those in math, should hold firm and true and not let you down. With some hard work on your part, some memorization of the formulas, you will be capable of some new musical ideas soon. Of this I am certain.

Since this book was going to be totally focused on lines and linear concepts, I knew that the play-along CD would have to be approached differently. For the former book, which dealt with chords and chordal harmony, you were supplied with play-along tracks that, in almost all cases, supplied you with only bass and percussion. Here you will find that you will still have the bass and percussion, but to give you a harmonic cushion, some harmonic support, you will hear string pads in the background on all the new tracks. This will give you the chance to hear your newly formed lines against something harmonically solid. And, in the end, knowing what you now sound like will give you that all-important sense of self-confidence for playing your lines in any context.

You will find on the CD a balance between recorded demonstrations of the written examples and many improvisations, which attempt to present the linear concepts as they could be used in real playing situations. Usually the demonstration track is immediately followed by the same track minus my guitar.

CONTEMPORARY CHORD KHANCEPTS shows you a complete and detailed description of my equipment on the "Technical Guitar Information" page (page 74). There was also a unique look into the recording process with Malcolm Pollack's "Engineering Notes" (page 75). For the recording of **PENTATONIC KHANCEPTS,** none of my guitar equipment really changed, and I still used my Gibson ES-335 ('82, from the Heritage Series) for everything. However, due to a problem I was having with one of my speakers (but it could have been something else!), we decided to mix the recording using only one side of my stereo sound; so the guitar, as you now hear it, appears in the center. On the engineering side, much of our recording process remained the same as well; though Malcolm had to improvise a bit since some of the outboard processing gear (reverb and delay units) in Al Gorgoni's studio had changed. Should you care to read about my equipment in greater detail, please feel free to visit the following Web page: **www.stevekhan.com/equipment.htm.** I am hopeful that one of these two sources will answer most of your questions about my musical equipment and the recording itself.

Steve Khan

For most of the tracks on the CD, I put to use one very simple yet solid even eighth-note rhythmic groove with a Latin flavor, which always appears at the moderate tempo of ♩ = 122. Though the groove may seem similar from track to track, the harmonic challenges are always different. Over some thirty years of private teaching, I've come to believe that this kind of play-along feel is the best way to connect with players from all genres, and that's a goal for this book.

For those of you who have always been jazz players, being forced to come to terms with playing over even eighth-note feels can be a great thing. For me, it remains difficult to get sequencers to feel like the brilliant playing of drummers such as Elvin Jones, Roy Haynes, Jack DeJohnette, Philly Joe Jones, and countless others. On "Hippity Hop to the Bebop Shop," **Tracks 3** and **4** on the CD, I decided to avoid these problems and present my version of a contemporary hip-hop shuffle beat that would allow the written passages to swing a bit. The tempo for these tracks is ♩ = 72. I am hopeful that this, in small part, will satisfy some of you from the jazz camp and inspire everyone else as well.

Though I am repeating myself, I can't stress enough that, in the long view, the linear approach presented in this book should work beautifully with the chordal and harmonic approach in **CONTEMPORARY CHORD KHANCEPTS.** During the performance of music, in any genre, your playing should always be a balance of all that you've experienced and learned so that it's not one-dimensional. If you allow yourself to do just the mental portion of this effort, learning the formulas as to why these pentatonics work so beautifully, I can guarantee that you will achieve results far faster than if you spend time resisting this aspect and just relying on your ears. True, in the end, everything will come down to your ear, your ability to hear something, but it's so important to understand why things do sound good. To that goal, I hope I can contribute something of lasting value to your music.

Stay safe and be well,

Steve Khan

New York City, October 2001

Original pen and ink by Jean-Michel Folon. Given to Steve as a gift for a possible songbook cover in 1980.
This particular drawing reminds us of Folon's painting for the *Tightrope* LP cover from '77.

Special Thanks

Al Gorgoni; Aaron Stang; Mike Selverne; Steven Laitmon; Christine Martin; Malcolm Pollack; Rob Mounsey; Felicia Michael; Ned Shaw; Blaine Fallis; Ron Aston; Christian Pacher; Oscar Hernández; Manolo Badrena; Marc Quiñones; Rubén Rodríguez; Willie Bobo; Piet Mondrian; Mike Landy; Kenny Inaoka; Patrizio Chiozza; Freddy Zerbib; Richard Laird; Rob Wallis; Colin Schofield; L. John Harris; Dennis Chambers; Anthony Jackson; Steve Jordan; Adam Gorgoni; Clare Fischer; Don Sebesky; Naoki Sawaoka; Nadine DeMarco; Dave Samuels; Rafael Greco; Alvaro Falcón: Daniel Ortíz; Angélica Lamarca Canelón; Doug West; Jean-Michel Folon; Heath Price-Khan; and to Caridad Canelón.

Acknowledgments

Gibson Guitars (Jimmy Archey, Lou Vito, and Darrell Gilbert); Dean Markley Strings (Dave Lienhard); Sadowsky Guitars (Roger Sadowsky); Walter Woods Amps (Walter Woods); Korg/Marshall (Mitch Colby); Yamaha Guitars (Shigenobu Miyake); Ibanez (John Lomas); LP/Latin Percussion (Martin Cohen); Danny K. Music Services; and Dreamhire.

Dedication

The work contained within this book is dedicated with love and respect to **DAN KELLER,** one of my dearest friends since junior high school, who recently passed away from lung cancer. If you are thinking about smoking, PLEASE don't ever start! If you are a smoker now, PLEASE do everything within your power to stop NOW!

Correspondence

Please feel free to visit my Web site: **http://www.stevekhan.com.**

And if you like, write to me anytime via the **CONTACT STEVE** page at the site.

Credits

Project Manager: Aaron Stang
Music Engraving and Book Layout/Design: Mark Burgess
Original Cover Design: Hélène Côté
Back Cover Illustration: Ned Shaw
Book Art Layout: Robert Ramsay
Photo of Steve Khan (page 5): Christian Pacher, Ingolstadt, Germany (May 31, 1993)
CD Recording Information:

Produced by:	Steve Khan
Associate Producers:	Al Gorgoni & Malcolm Pollack
Programmed & Sequenced by:	Steve Khan & Al Gorgoni
Additional Sequencing:	Steve Khan & Rob Mounsey
Recorded at:	Lightstream Studios, N.Y.C., NY - October 20–21, 2001
Recorded and Mixed by:	Malcolm Pollack
Post-Production:	Rob Mounsey @ Flying Monkey Studios
Flying Monkey Assistant:	Felicia Michael

TABLE OF CONTENTS

Steve Khan

Page CDTrack

UNIT ONE
Pentatonic Scales: What Are They?

The definition of a pentatonic scale according to the HARVARD DICTIONARY OF MUSIC is the following:

> **A scale of five different pitches.** One form can be played by sounding six successive black keys of the piano (the sixth constitutes an octave of the first and does not count as a different pitch). The pentatonic scale is commonly found worldwide, including indigenous American music, Eastern Europe, the Far East, and Africa. Variations of the pentatonic scale are also found in black gospel music and rhythm and blues.

In the world of improvised popular music, I believe that the pentatonic scale has become synonymous with any grouping of five notes. And those notes, as a unit, do not have to have anything to do with a particular chord sound or name. As was stated above, there can be some very exotic and unusual pentatonic scales. With this point in mind, let's begin exploring this concept.

For improvised music, we are going to use only two pentatonic configurations. Both can be derived from any major key, though they would begin from different starting notes (pitches, tones, degrees, or voices). In the key of F major, for example, the Dorian mode is built upon the second degree, which would give us G Dorian (G, A, B♭, C, D, E, F). This mode is most commonly used for extended improvisations (solos, jams) over a Gm7 chord or perhaps the closely related C7 chord. For the minor pentatonic, we would extract five of the seven modal notes. In this sample key, we would omit the notes E and A. We are then left with the basic **minor pentatonic,** which would always contain the root **(R)**; minor third **(m3rd)**; fourth **(4th)**; fifth **(5th)**; and seventh **(7th)** degrees.

You may be familiar with this grouping of notes but have been thinking of it as the **major pentatonic** but built from the relative major of G minor, which, in this case, would be B♭ major pentatonic. A basic major pentatonic always presents us with the root **(R),** second **(2nd),** third **(3rd),** fifth **(5th),** and sixth **(6th)** degrees. In each case, the degrees remain the same; it's just a matter of consolidating your points of orientation. See the chart below:

Minor Pentatonic	R	m3rd	4th	5th	7th
G minor pentatonic	G	B♭	C	D	F
Major Pentatonic	**R**	**2nd**	**3rd**	**5th**	**6th**
B♭ major pentatonic	B♭	C	D	F	G

As you can see, the notes are in fact the same. So, I am hoping that while working through the materials in the book, you will buy into my concept, my point of orientation, and choose to relate to everything by using either the minor pentatonic or a second pentatonic I am about to introduce.

Steve Khan

In the example key of F major, the Mixolydian mode is built upon the 5th degree, which would give us C Mixolydian (C, D, E, F, G, A, B♭). Generally speaking, and from the perspective of the root, this mode is used for extended improvisations over stationary (static) **dominant 7th chords,** in this case C7. To arrive at the basic dominant 7th pentatonic, we would again put to use five of the seven modal notes, here leaving out only F and A. This gives us a configuration using the root **(R),** second **(2nd),** third **(3rd),** fifth **(5th),** and seventh **(7th).**

Dominant 7th Pentatonic	R	2nd	3rd	5th	7th
C dominant 7th pentatonic	C	D	E	G	B♭
Minor Pentatonic	R	m3rd	4th	5th	7th
G minor pentatonic	G	B♭	C	D	F

Mixolydian Pentatonic R1 3 4 5 / C E F G B♭

The harmonic relationship between Gm7 and C7 as a iim7-V7 should be obvious, and the pentatonics, which we've derived, are just as closely related. In fact, of the five notes used for each, four are exactly the same. The only difference is that the G minor pentatonic uses an F and the C dominant 7th pentatonic uses an E. In the flow of moving lines, this small difference can prove to be a great addition to the sound and shape of your lines. As full modes, G Dorian (Gm7) and C Mixolydian (C7) contain exactly the same seven notes, all derived from the key of F major.

The dominant 7th pentatonic is not something I discovered through my college music studies, private teachers, or even shared exchanges of information with other musicians. I came upon it through my studies of pianist McCoy Tyner's improvisations, especially those found on his recordings as part of John Coltrane's legendary quartet (Coltrane, Tyner, bassist Jimmy Garrison, and drummer Elvin Jones) for Impulse Records during the mid-'60s. Due to the close relationship between the minor pentatonic and the blues scale, it was relatively easy to detect McCoy's usage of the minor pentatonic, but the more I listened, I kept hearing another configuration of notes. After many more hours of sitting in front of the stereo, I was finally able to define this five-note grouping and realized that it, too, conformed to the diatonic structures, but that it began on the 5th degree of the major scale (this being the degree of the dominant 7th). So, from that point forward, I have always referred to this scale as the dominant 7th pentatonic.

USING THE CD: Once you've been able to get the following fingerings to a reasonable level of readiness, you can begin to try to apply them by practicing playing them slowly over **Track 2** on the CD. It's a C pedal shuffle at a moderate tempo and should enable you to hear just what both a G minor pentatonic and a C dominant 7th pentatonic sound like over this particular root. I have chosen the root of the V7 chord because it enhances the sounds produced by the iim pentatonic, in this case, G minor pentatonic. You can also practice these same two pentatonics over **Track 24,** which is a simple G pedal, but this time you are playing over an even eighth-note pulse.

Example 1: Minor Pentatonic Fingerings
Example: G Minor
Key of: F Major
Mode: G Dorian

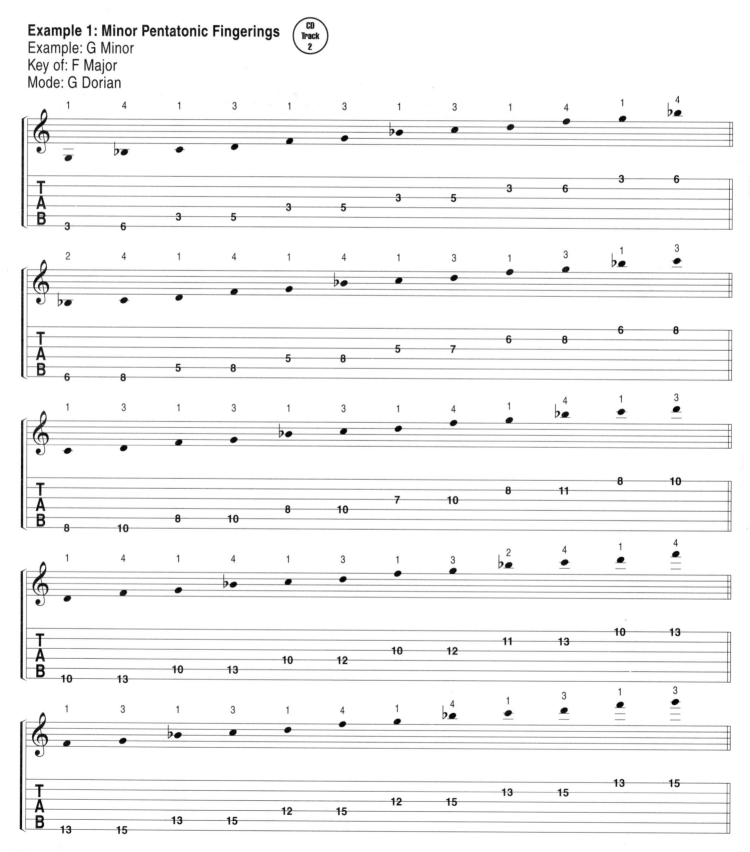

Steve Khan

USING THE CD: Just as with the previous minor pentatonic fingerings, once you've been able to get the dominant 7th pentatonic to a reasonable level of readiness, try to apply them by playing them slowly over **Track 2** on the CD. You can also practice the C dominant 7th pentatonic over **Track 24,** a simple G pedal, which would allow you to hear how it might sound over a G minor sonority.

Example 2: Dominant 7th Pentatonic Fingerings
Example: C7
Key of: F Major
Mode: C Mixolydian

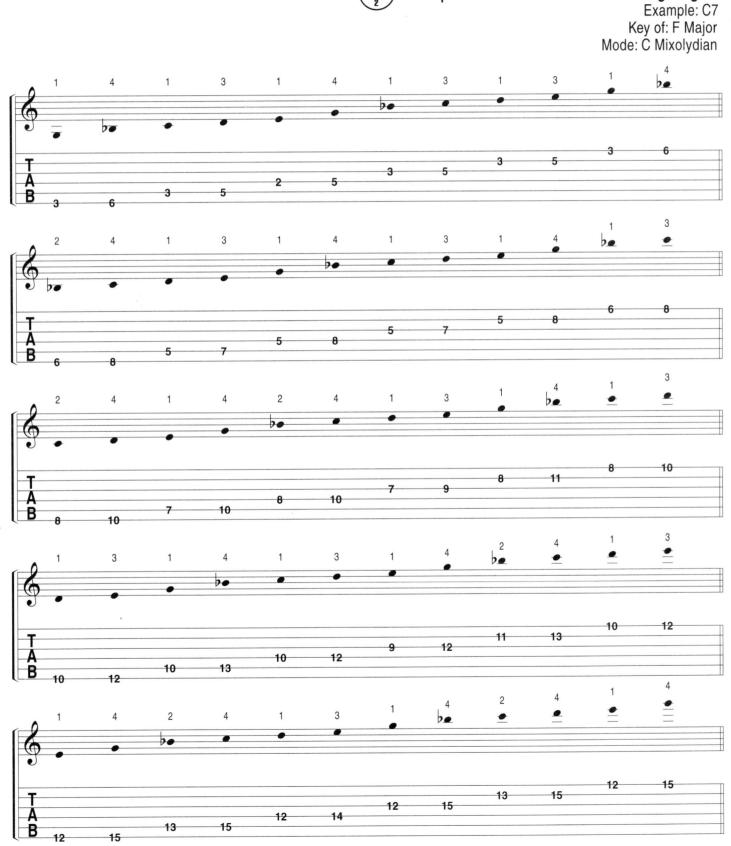

UNIT TWO
Relationship of the Minor Pentatonic to the Blues Scale

One of my principal reasons for presenting the materials and concepts in this book is to help all players find a closer connection between the blues and more sophisticated forms of harmony. Often times when a player is confronted by a chord, other than a dominant 7th or minor 7th chord, any relation to the blues or to a kind of "bluesiness" can seem rather foreign when, in fact, it could be right at his or her fingertips. Perhaps the first step to breaking down these barriers is to examine the relationship of the minor pentatonic to the blues scale of the same root.

This example shoes G as the root:

G minor pentatonic	R	m3rd		4th		5th	7th
	G	B♭		C		D	F
G blues scale	R	m3rd	3rd*	4th	♭5th	5th	7th
	G	B♭ (blue note)	B	C	C♯/D♭ (blue note)	D	F

* This pitch can appear as a microtone between B♭ and B♮.

Upon closer inspection, it becomes clear that there is essentially a one-note, one-and-a-half-note, or two-note difference between these two scales. How you learn to use the blue notes and that subtle microtone will really keep your improvisations closely tied to the roots, the common ground—the blues! You will be able to do this by simply adding the notes from the blues scale to the minor pentatonic you chose to employ over any one of the chord families discussed. Once you've mastered the theories behind using the minor pentatonics, you can begin to add the blues scale and all of its nuances, which only the guitar seems to offer.

Example 3: G Minor Pentatonic

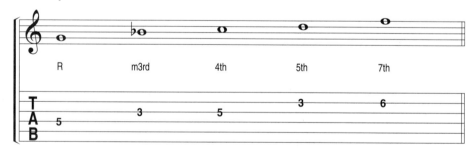

G Blues Scale

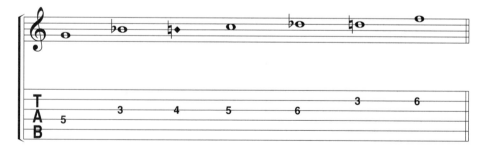

For those of you who are new to improvising through complex sets of chord changes from musical experiences in rock, R&B, or country, I feel that it would only be fair to provide an example of jazz-oriented lines. It's important to do this so you can see and hear the significant differences in the shapes and sounds of these lines as opposed to the pentatonic lines from which this book draws its focus.

Jazz lines not only observe the basic principles of sounding out a scale or mode per each chord family and change, but also, within the number of beats allowed, the basic modal/scale tones can be, and are, embellished by the usage of upper and lower neighbors (both chromatic and consonant), chromatic passing tones, simple arpeggios, and occasional idiosyncratic rhythmic groupings. Even with all of these elements adding to the quality and character of the lines, there still exists a decidedly scale-oriented quality to the shape of the lines. In other words, one note follows the next in relatively close proximity. Like any genre, jazz has its own language, and to play it in a recognizable way requires that you learn to speak this language.

Using pentatonic scales in your improvising vocabulary, while dropping only two notes from the diatonic scales or modes, will give your lines a decidedly more angular sound, look, and feel. But, perhaps more than this, by truly understanding and hearing the relationship between the minor pentatonic and the blues scale, as previously addressed, it will add an earthiness to your playing that perhaps had been missing. In a strange way, what I have just said could really be mostly addressed to those of you who are already competent jazz players. As a listener in recent years, I find that this quality is sadly missing from many young and very sophisticated players. By the same token, there are many rock-fusion players—with technical gifts I could only hope to achieve someday—who have, in their way, already mastered the art of flying around the fingerboard in pentatonic flurries, but those players seem to have missed the soulful element where the blues is connected to everything. It's my sincere hope that some of the concepts, put forth in these pages, will help and inspire players from all styles to hear great things.

Many years ago, long, LONG before the birth of the smooth jazz genre, when I was part of the Brecker Bros. Band, we had arguably the greatest small horn section in existence, with Randy Brecker (trumpet), Michael Brecker (tenor sax), and David Sanborn (alto sax). And, in those years, the '70s, all of us in the band were constantly amazed at how, after the brilliant and complex improvisations of both Randy and Michael, Dave Sanborn could play over the same chord changes and capture something so very different. He could somehow hear through all the complex chord changes (especially those in the compositions of Randy Brecker) and go immediately to where the bluesiness existed. He did this no matter how sophisticated an individual chord or series of chord changes might have been. It was a great lesson for us all. This is to say that you could still be deeply committed to one particular style of playing, not lose any of that, but add some degree of depth and sophistication to your playing. For others, you might need to realize that, at times, **simple is best.**

Example 4: "Hippity Hop to the Bebop Shop" (ii-V-I-VI7, in E♭)

USING THE CD: Presented over a contemporary hip-hop shuffle groove, "Hippity Hop to the Bebop Shop" presents a mini-compendium of jazz lines and jazz mannerisms. I don't believe that anyone would ever play such a thing in the context of a real improvisation or solo, but again, for the purposes of this book, I am simply trying to share as much as I can in the space given. So, you can watch **Example 4** go by and listen to **Track 3** and you will then hear a full 32 bars of lines played in a pretty traditional jazz style. At **bar 33** and through the fade, you will then hear that I switched to a pentatonic style of playing, and it is my feeling that you'll be struck by the radical difference between the two approaches. You should hear that the pentatonic lines sound much more angular and disjointed than the jazz lines. At least this was my intent. Also of special note is the time feel for playing either style of line where swing is perhaps more important than the notes. You will hear that I played with a rather lazy or laid-back time feel on purpose, trying to play a bit behind the beat and then, without making it too noticeable, catching up to the pulse. Please make an effort to give this a try too. It can make such a huge difference in how your playing is perceived and felt by others. It has much to do with developing a high level of rhythmic self-confidence. When you feel ready to play the written example or to attempt your own improvisations, use **Track 4.**

Example 4: "Hippity Hop to the Bebop Shop"

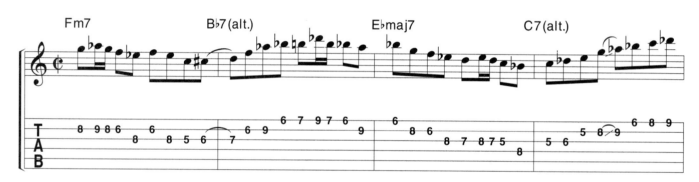

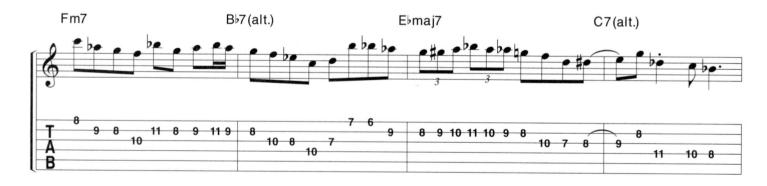

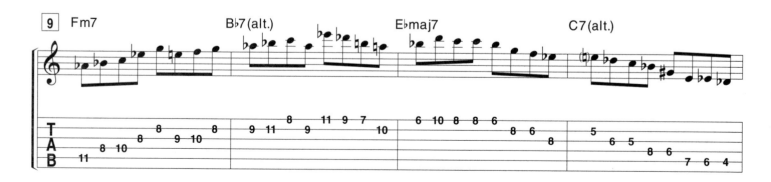

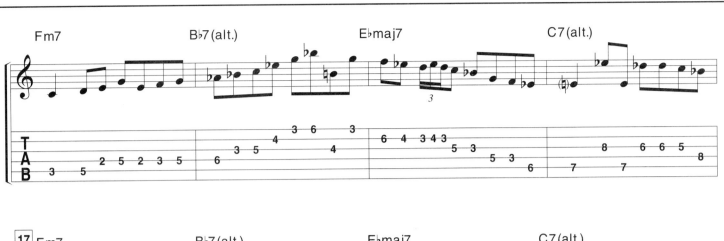

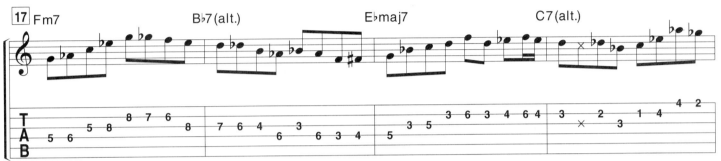

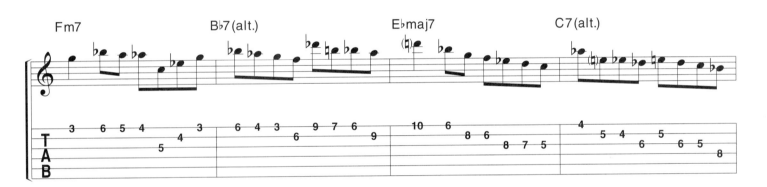

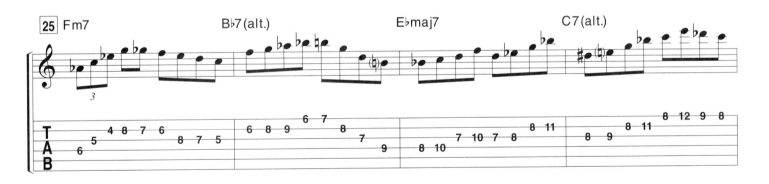

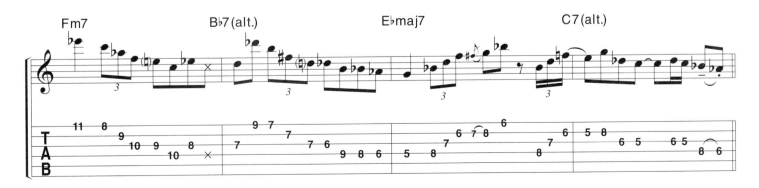

Pentatonic Khancepts

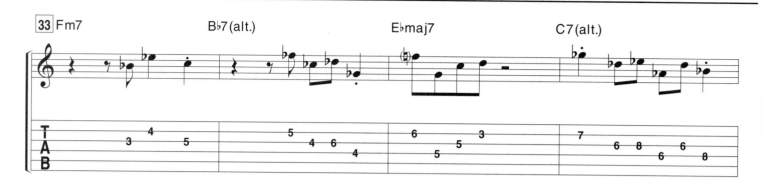

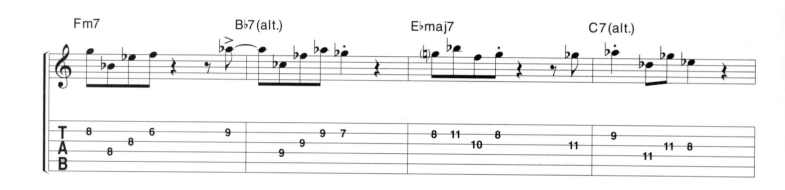

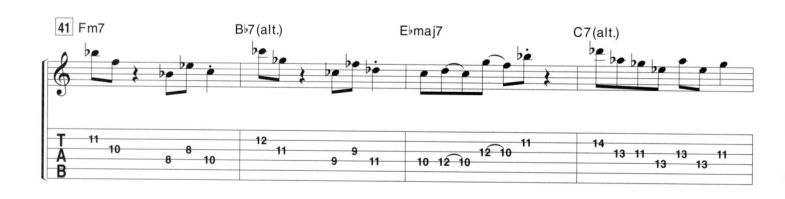

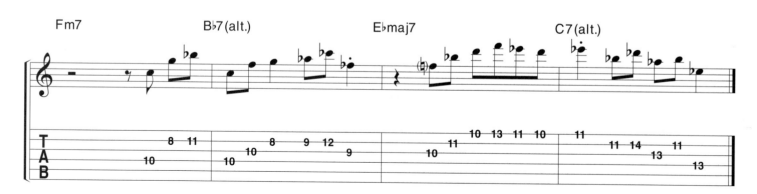

Steve Khan

This is where the theoretical and/or mathematical-oriented section of this work really begins. What I tried to do for myself many years ago was to find a way to put some kind of order to **how, where,** and **when** I could apply these two fundamental pentatonic scales (the minor and the dominant 7th pentatonics) to most of the commonly used chord forms (or chord families as I like to call them) that we encounter on a daily basis in the music we play.

I began by taking the three most basic chord forms and families—**MAJOR, MINOR,** and **DOMINANT**—and sought to apply those two pentatonics to see just what I could come up with. In addition, I realized that the **m7(b5)** chord form, since it is part of the diatonic family of scales, was a possibility too. And finally, to be able to use these pentatonic scales over the sophistication of **altered dominant 7th** chords as they resolve to major and minor would be an invaluable tool.

The units that follow address each of these chord forms and families and present one sample chord form in one key. It will supply you with all the pentatonic possibilities and in some cases make suggestions, from my experience, just which ones will sound best and in which contexts or genres.

To communicate these options to you in the most efficient manner, I have used grids or tables that show you the options you might have AND just which color tones they produce against the given chord form. You may simply find that they sound good, and that will be enough. You will go on and apply them as you choose. But some of you might want to understand just what it is you're doing and **why** it might sound so good and so appealing to your ears. Either way, the materials, the tools, are there for you and presented in a very clear and efficient manner.

When viewing any of these grids, you will find that to the immediate right of each pentatonic listed you are presented with the notes in that particular minor or dominant 7th pentatonic. Above each of those notes is the scale degree that that note produces relative to the root of the chord form being discussed in that unit/chapter. This same principle of presentation applies to all the chord families that follow. With a cursory look, you can immediately see which pentatonics are giving you the most color tones—those notes above the root, 3rd, and 5th.

Beyond all the theory, the math, and the memorization, what is most important for your growth is developing a personal and emotional relationship with the notes you choose to play. Some of the more gifted among you will simply hear things and will be guided by that instinct. Others will have to search and work very hard at finding it. I suggest the following approach when you begin to improvise over the play-along tracks for each of the chord families.

Before I get to the specifics, I think that this is the appropriate moment to mention something directly related to the guitar. As guitarists, we should remember that when we play, we are playing one of the most visually "naked" instruments. That is to say, people who come to **hear** us play often times are unfortunately **listening with their eyes, not with their ears.** We want people to **hear** the music. But we live in a visual age, and getting people to hear the music is hard to do. On the guitar it is obvious when we go up or down the neck; when a particular motif goes up or down in sequence, it's apparent to the audience. Ultimately, beyond one's technical abilities and speed, what audiences truly remember are moments of great lyricism, great improvised melodies, and the **interplay** with the other musicians. Please strive for these elements perhaps more than becoming the world's greatest virtuoso. It is not a calling for many!

Unit Four

First, **always begin by playing slowly.** An element that might help give you a grounding before you begin to improvise lines would be simply to find a chordal groove that sits well within these play-along tracks. The examples I have improvised for you begin in that fashion. Beginning with something chordal helped set the mood and put me within the time feel of the accompaniment. Each play-along in the following units was recorded with a metronome marking of ♩ = 122, which is a nice medium tempo for all players. And it is offered with an even eighth-note feel and a Latin attitude so that it can appeal to both jazz and pop players.

When you feel ready to improvise lines, try to begin by simply staying in one area of the instrument, an area in which you feel you have the greatest touch, tone, and sensitivity. Then, since the pentatonic scale has only five notes, try to work with just three of those notes. Try surrounding one of these three notes (which you could choose beforehand) using the other two to make that one note more expressive. Try the notes with vibrato and without, with a sharp attack from your right hand, and with a soft or dull attack. But the main thing is to listen and to **feel** what your reaction is when **you** play **that note** against the chordal sonority. Does playing that particular note reach you in some way? For example, what does it feel like to you to play a G or a C or a B♭ against the E♭ major 7 sounds?

A thorough exploration could take some time, and you must allow yourself that time. I hope that this doesn't sound like too distant a goal, but perhaps from the day you begin, allow yourself some time, maybe several weeks, maybe as much as six months, and see where you can be with daily improvising in this one area. It's an individual process, and what works for one of you may not work for another. Just go at your own pace. Let that be your guide always. Steady wins the race!

With this said, let's move on to the five chord families offered.

Steve with his honey sunburst Les Paul ca. '82.
Used on Donald Fagen's *True Companion*.

C Maj7   E, A, B minor Pent

> **MAJOR CHORDS:** On any major chord, the player **may apply minor pentatonics** built upon the **3rd, 6th,** or **7th degrees** of the Ionian mode (the major scale) or Lydian mode. Other options in certain contexts might include the minor pentatonic built upon the 2nd degree and the dominant 7th pentatonic built upon the 2nd degree.

For example, over E♭maj7 use:

G minor pentatonic	3rd G	5th B♭	6th C	maj7th D	9th F
D minor pentatonic	maj7th D	9th F	3rd G	♯4 A	6th C
C minor pentatonic	6th C	[R] E♭	9th F	3rd G	5th B♭
Other options:					
F minor pentatonic	2nd F	[4th] A♭	5th B♭	6th C	[R] E♭
F dom. 7th pentatonic	2nd F	3rd G	♯4 A	6th C	[R] E♭

MAJOR CHORDS

In the context of progressive instrumental music (jazz and jazz-rock fusion), I recommend the minor pentatonics built upon the 3rd and the 7th degrees of the major scale (Ionian mode) because they afford the nicest selection of color tones. In addition, because of the configurations of the tones in any minor pentatonic, there exists a subtlety in how the notes fall against the chord and its sound.

Often, players discovering the beauties of the sharp-fourth (♯4) in major chords tend to overemphasize that note rather than allowing it to happen as the improvised line unveils itself. By using the minor pentatonic built upon the 7th (the major 7th), it introduces this tone and presents it with some degree of subtlety.

With major chords appearing in rock, country, R & B, and folk styles, the minor pentatonic built upon the 6th degree can, and does, sound fine. To hard-core players and listeners alike, there is usually no danger of sounding too jazzy, which is a common complaint. However, with more jazz-based music, you'll find that you have to be a little more careful when using this pentatonic. It's the presence of the root [R] that can cause a kind of friction, even a dissonance, because it can rub against the major 7th within the chord. You'll find that players like Wes Montgomery and George Benson, plus all of those influenced by them, use this minor pentatonic to give their lines a bluesy flavor by skating over or just by the root and not making that degree appear so pronounced in the line. They also do this by adding tones from the blues scale to the minor pentatonic built upon the 6th degree.

I'd be remiss if I didn't present two other pentatonics listed in the pentatonic theory chart section. These pentatonics contain the technically correct notes, but to my ears they also can present problems. One option is the minor pentatonic built upon the 2nd degree, giving you the 2nd or 9th; 4th; 5th; 6th; and [R]. The problems can arise because of the inclusion of the 4th (the suspension) and, of course, the root. Let the style of music and your ears dictate just how usable this pentatonic might be for you. It's also possible to use a dominant 7th pentatonic built upon the 2nd degree, which produces the 2nd or 9th; 3rd; ♯4th; 6th; and [R]. Again, a problem occurs because of the presence of the root [R]. Also, because of the presence of the ♯4th, which gives it a Lydian feeling, this pentatonic will probably sound best in more jazz-oriented settings.

MAJOR CHORD REFERENCE CHART

CHORD	MINOR PENT. [3rd]	MINOR PENT. [6th]	MINOR PENT. [7th]	MINOR PENT. [2nd]	DOM. 7 PENT. [2nd]
Cmaj7	**E**	A	**B**	D	D
D♭maj7	**F**	B♭	**C**	E♭	E♭
Dmaj7	**F#**	B	**C#**	E	E
E♭maj7	**G**	C	**D**	F	F
Emaj7	**G#**	C#	**D#**	F#	F#
F maj7	**A**	D	**E**	G	G
G♭maj7	**B♭**	E♭	**F**	A♭	A♭
Gmaj7	**B**	E	**F#**	A	A
A♭maj7	**C**	F	**G**	B♭	B♭
Amaj7	**C#**	F#	**G#**	B	B
B♭maj7	**D**	G	**A**	C	C
Bmaj7	**D#**	G#	**A#**	C#	C#

USING THE CD: You can hear the performed version of **Example 5** by playing **Track 5** on the CD. With all the examples I performed for the individual chord families, I tried to first play something that puts me in the rhythmic groove of the track; then the improvisation begins simply using, in varying ways, many of the available pentatonics. In addition, I try to use the blues language as well so that we are never too far removed from that. When you are ready to attempt your own improvisations, use **Track 6.**

Example 5: On Major Chords (E♭maj7)

Pentatonic Khancepts

Dmi7 = D, E, A minor pent

> **MINOR CHORDS:** On any minor chord, the player **may apply minor pentatonics** built upon the **root, 2nd,** and **5th degrees** of the Dorian mode and the **dominant 7th pentatonic** built upon the **4th.**

For example, over Em7 use:

E minor pentatonic	R E	m3rd G	4th A	5th B	7th D
F# minor pentatonic	9th F#	4th A	5th B	6th C#	R E
B minor pentatonic	5th B	7th D	R E	9th F#	4th A
A dom. 7th pentatonic	4th A	5th B	6th C#	R E	m3rd G

MINOR CHORDS

Of all the chord families addressed in this book, the minor chord family is the one that already exists in minor. So, there's no need to convert the thinking part because you would simply use the Dorian mode built from the root. In the example of Em7, we would use the E Dorian mode. The use of the three minor pentatonics is very straightforward and should come down to a simple matter of taste. You would use just those containing notes you really hear. All three, in my opinion, are going to sound terrific. The minor pentatonics built upon the root and 5th degrees only differ in that the one built from the 5th degree does not use the m3rd and therefore offers greater subtlety. It also adds the color tone of the 9th, which some find to be a very pretty note. The minor pentatonic built upon the 2nd degree also gives you the 9th, and, in addition to that, presents the color tone of the 6th. It, too, is a pretty note, but not one to be overused. You should always feel free to try to use all of these pentatonics because experience will tell you which ones fit into your personal style.

However, this is an excellent place to begin to get accustomed to using the dominant 7th pentatonic. With the example of Em7, the modal orientation being E Dorian, we are in the key of D major, so Em7 is a ii chord, and A7 would be a V7 chord. The A dominant 7th pentatonic is built from the 4th degree of E Dorian, and it only differs from the E minor pentatonic in that it has a C# (6th or 13th) instead of D (the 7th). While getting familiar with this sound, try interchanging the E minor pentatonic and the A dominant 7th pentatonic to hear the color change created by this one-note difference when you play along with the CD. In **Example 6** you should pay attention to **bars 24–25** and **29–30** offered as a point of reference.

Steve Khan

MINOR CHORD REFERENCE CHART

CHORD	MINOR PENT. [R]	MINOR PENT. [2nd]	MINOR PENT. [5th]	DOM. 7TH PENT. [4th]
Cm7	C	D	G	F
D♭m7	D♭	E♭	A♭	G♭
Dm7	D	E	A	G
E♭m7	E♭	F	B♭	A♭
Em7	E	F#	B	A
Fm7	F	G	C	B♭
F#m7/G♭m7	F#/G♭	G#/A♭	C#/D♭	B/C♭
Gm7	G	A	D	C
A♭m7	A♭	B♭	E♭	D♭
Am7	A	B	E	D
B♭m7	B♭	C	F	E♭
Bm7	B	C#	F#	E

USING THE CD: To hear **Example 6** performed, simply go to **Track 7** on the CD. The approach is much the same as it was for the major chord family section in **Unit Five.** When you're ready to begin to experiment with your own improvisations, use **Track 8,** which omits my guitar.

Example 6: On Minor Chords (Em7)

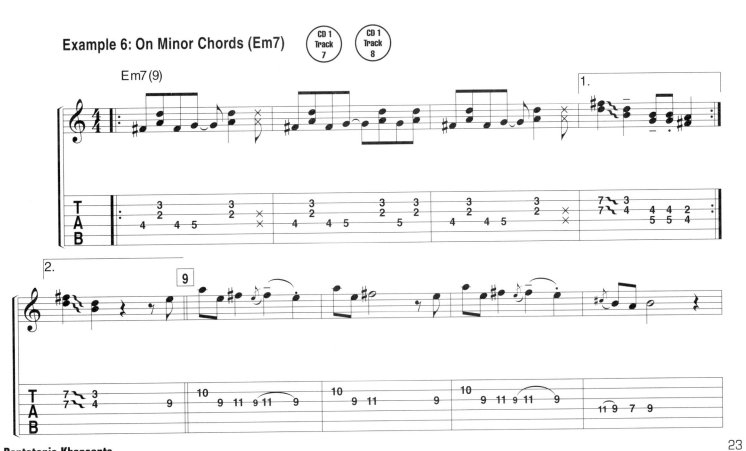

Steve Khan

> **DOMINANT 7TH CHORDS:** On any stationary dominant 7th chord, the player **may apply minor pentatonics** built upon the **2nd, 5th,** and **6th degrees** of the Mixolydian mode and **dominant 7th pentatonics** built upon the **root** and **2nd degrees.**

For example, over A7(9) use:

E minor pentatonic	5th E	7th G	R A	9th B	4th D
F♯ minor pentatonic	6th F♯	R A	9th B	3rd C♯	5th E
B minor pentatonic	9th B	4th D	5th E	6th F♯	R A
A dom. 7th pentatonic	R A	9th B	3rd C♯	5th E	7th G
B dom. 7th pentatonic	9th B	3rd C♯	♭5th D♯	6th F♯	R A

DOMINANT 7TH CHORDS

For a stationary dominant 7th chord, which is not going to resolve to either a I major or a i minor chord, the correct mode to use is Mixolydian. However, in my minor (Dorian) orientation, I would employ the Dorian mode built upon the 5th degree of the Mixolydian mode. In the example of A9, the 5th degree is E, so I would be relating to this as E Dorian.

Looking at the pentatonic options, the dominant 7th pentatonic built upon the root offers only one color tone, the 9th. The minor pentatonic built upon the 5th degree extends the harmony further by having the 9th and adding the 4th or 11th (the suspension). In some R&B and gospel music, as well as jazz, which has been influenced by those genres, the minor pentatonic built upon the 6th degree offers a bluesiness in a most subtle way. Obviously you could employ the A blues scale if that's what you heard. Finally, the dominant 7th pentatonic built upon the 2nd degree extends the harmony the furthest as it introduces the ♯4 or ♭5 to the color scheme. Sometimes, if the mood strikes, I just play the blues scale one whole step above the root to accentuate this feeling. In **Example 7,** you would want to listen to **bars 23–24** and **27–30.**

DOMINANT 7TH CHORD REFERENCE CHART

CHORD	MINOR PENT. [5th]	MINOR PENT. [6th]	MINOR PENT. [2nd]	DOM. 7TH PENT. [R]	DOM. 7TH PENT. [2nd]
C7	G	A	D	C	D
D♭7	A♭	B♭	E♭	D♭	E♭
D7	A	B	E	D	E
E♭7	B♭	C	F	E♭	F
E7	B	C#	F#	E	F#
F7	C	D	G	F	G
F#7/G♭7	C#/D♭	D#/E♭	G#/A♭	F#/G♭	G#/A♭
G7	D	E	A	G	A
A♭7	E♭	F	B♭	A♭	B♭
A7	E	F#	B	A	B
B♭7	F	G	C	B♭	C
B7	F#	G#	C#	B	C#

USING THE CD: To hear **Example 7** performed, play **Track 9** on the CD. When you're ready to use the suggested pentatonics and begin to experience what you hear, use **Track 10.**

Example 7: On Dominant 7th Chords (A7)

Steve Khan

UNIT EIGHT
Minor 7(♭5) or Half-diminshed Chords

> **MINOR 7(♭5) or HALF-DIMINISHED CHORDS:** On any minor 7(♭5) (aka half-dimin-ished chord) the player **may apply minor pentatonics** built upon the **m3rd, 4th,** or **7th degrees** of the Locrian mode and the **dominant 7th pentatonic** built upon the **6th degree.**

For example, over Am7(♭5) use:

C minor pentatonic	m3rd C	♭5 E♭	6th F	7th G	2nd B♭
D minor pentatonic	4th D	6th F	7th G	R A	m3rd C
G minor pentatonic	7th G	2nd B♭	m3rd C	4th D	6th F
F dom. 7th pentatonic	6th F	7th G	R A	m3rd C	♭5 E♭

MINOR 7(♭5) CHORDS

The minor 7(♭5) (or half-diminished 7th chord) can appear to be and even sound like a stranger to the diatonic scale, but it is, in fact, the scale degree of the major 7th and sug-gests the Locrian mode, which is one of the seven diatonic modes. In my orientation, I choose to view this as the Dorian mode, a minor 3rd (m3rd) above the root. So, here in our example of Am7(♭5), I would think of this as C Dorian! As it turns out, my favorite minor pentatonic to use over m7(♭5) chords is built from the minor 3rd as well, C minor pentatonic.

Of special note is the minor pentatonic built from the 7th degree. For our example chord, that would be G minor pentatonic. Were we to look at the long-range function of the m7(♭5), we would see it as the first part of a iim7(♭5) - V7(alt.) - im7 progression. So, a fully real-ized cadence in this key would become Am7(♭5) - D7(alt.) - Gm7. Often, in blues groups and jazz-oriented blues groups (like the classic organ trio: organ-guitar-drums), you'll hear the soloists playing through this entire blues cadence using the blues scale of the root. Here, the G blues scale, which closely resembles our G minor pentatonic, becomes our option of choice. For these same reasons, this is the way in which this pentatonic can sound good over a m7(♭5) chord when it is isolated and not functioning as a part of a cadential progression.

MINOR 7(♭5) CHORD REFERENCE CHART

CHORD	MINOR PENT. [m3rd]	MINOR PENT. [4th]	MINOR PENT. [7th]	DOM. 7TH PENT. [6th]
Cm7(♭5)	E♭	F	B♭	A♭
D♭m7(♭5)	E/F♭	G♭	C♭	A
Dm7(♭5)	F	G	C	B♭
E♭m7(♭5)	G♭	A♭	D♭	B
Em7(♭5)	G	A	D	C
Fm7(♭5)	A♭	B♭	E♭	D♭
F#m7(♭5)/G♭m7(♭5)	A/B♭♭	B/C♭	E/F♭	D
Gm7(♭5)	B♭	C	F	E♭
A♭m7(♭5)	B/C♭	D♭	G♭	E
Am7(♭5)	C	D	G	F
B♭m7(♭5)	D♭	E♭	A♭	G♭
Bm7(♭5)	D	E	A	G

USING THE CD: To hear the recorded version of **Example 8,** play **Track 11.** When you feel ready to improvise, use **Track 12.**

Example 8: On m7(♭5) Chords

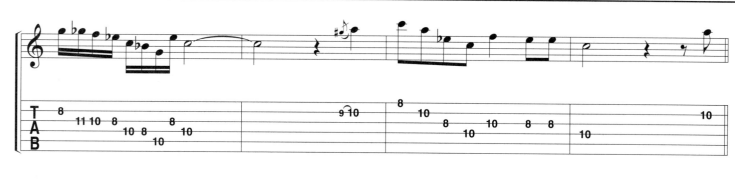

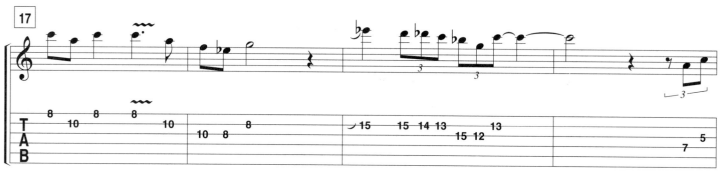

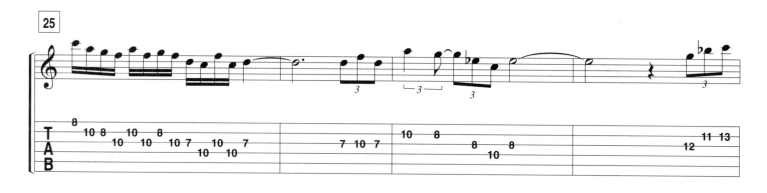

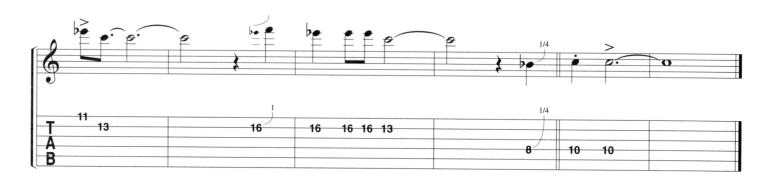

Steve Khan

> **ALTERED DOMINANT 7TH CHORDS:** On almost any altered dominant 7th chord, the player **may apply minor pentatonics** built upon the **#9** or 7th degrees of the altered dominant scale (Super Locrian mode) and **dominant 7th pentatonics** built upon the **♭5** or **#5.**

For example over C7(alt.) use:

E♭ minor pentatonic	#9 E♭	♭5 G♭	#5 A♭	7th B♭	♭9 D♭
G♭ dom. 7th pentatonic	♭5 G♭	#5 A♭	7th B♭	♭9 D♭	3rd F♭
A♭ dom. 7th pentatonic	#5 A♭	7th B♭	R C	#9 E♭	♭5 G♭
Other options:					
B♭ minor pentatonic	7th B♭	♭9 D♭	#9 E♭	[4th] F	#5 A♭

ALTERED DOMINANT 7TH CHORDS

As I initially learned it, the correct scale to apply to any altered dominant 7th chord is the altered dominant scale, which is made up of: root [R], ♭9, #9, 3rd, ♭5, #5, 7th. It contains all four of the possible altered tones (♭5, #5, ♭9, #9). With today's modern improvising systems and strategies, many players choose to call these same pitches the Super Locrian mode. Others, like me, end up relating to this problem by thinking of it as the melodic minor scale one half step above the root. So, in the example of C7(alt.), you might choose to think of this as D♭ melodic minor. If you're having a problem seeing this, just spell out all three scales (modes) and you should find that they have the same notes, though some may be enharmonically spelled.

C altered dominant	R C	♭9 D♭	#9 E♭	3rd **E**	♭5 G♭	#5 **G#**	7th B♭
D♭ melodic minor	C	D♭	E♭	**F♭**	G♭	**A♭**	B♭

The use of the altered dominant scale might only be problematic when you are confronted with a dominant 7th chord with the natural 13th, which also contains alterations. Using the example chord of C7(alt.), the form I am speaking of would be C13(♭9). When you are faced with a 13(♭9) chord, this is one of the few times when the half-tone/whole-tone diminished scale (from the root) should be used since it gives you both the natural 6th/13th and the ♭9.

Of the four pentatonics offered, the one built upon the #9 is the only one that contains all four altered tones (♭5, #5, ♭9, #9) and, for obvious reasons, it should be one of your first and best choices. I believe that you'll also find the two dominant 7th pentatonics built up from the ♭5 and the #5 to be very useful since they contain three of the four altered tones each. Often we hear players employ a Phrygian sound over the altered dominant 7th chord by simply playing the Dorian mode one whole step below the root. Here, over a C7(alt.) chord, B♭ Dorian would be played and would give you the C Phrygian mode.

C altered dominant	C	D♭	E♭	E	G♭	G#	B♭
B♭ Dorian/ C Phrygian	C	D♭	E♭	4th [F]	5th [G]	A♭	B♭

Unit Nine

For those of you with a background in classical music harmony and theory, what really takes place when you employ this device is the creation of a plagal cadence, sometimes referred to as the "Amen" cadence, IV-I and/or iv/I. Using the example chord as part of a full cadence, you could derive something like this:

Gm7	C7(altered)	Fmaj7
G Dorian	C altered dominant	F major/Lydian
Gm7	**B♭m7/C**	**Fmaj7**
G Dorian	B♭ Dorian	F major/Lydian

Breaking it down in this manner for analysis makes sense, but your ears and musical sensibilities must make the real choices. Carrying this out even further by using the minor pentatonic built upon the 7th degree, presented as an option, you could use the B♭ minor pentatonic. It offers, to my ears, one problem note—the 4th, the suspension—which, when played against an altered dominant 7th chord, does not create enough tension, and the 4th can actually sound like a wrong note. However, if you skillfully work your way around that one note, this minor pentatonic can sound fine.

Unlike the preceding chord families addressed in **Units 5–8,** to sustain an altered dominant 7th chord for a prolonged amount of time, two to three minutes, is just not practical or realistic. Doing so would seriously test some of my fundamental beliefs about the make-up of good music. That is to say, in the making of good music, [1] you can't really just have everything sound consonant; otherwise, it will get very, very boring. Likewise, [2] you can't have all tension because that can become just as tedious. So, as with many things in life, one must achieve a balance, leading to the creation of tension and then its eventual release upon resolution. All great music has these elements in their own particular balance.

During my improvised example, **Track 13,** "Frontier Justice," and the play-along, **Track 14,** that follows, you are given eight bars of our example chord, C7(alt.), which then resolves to six (6) different chordal areas. This gives you the opportunity to create pentatonic lines over various altered dominant sonorities, supplied by the string pads, and then you are asked to resolve those lines to different harmonic areas. Those areas include both the expected and the unexpected. The expected are resolutions to Fmaj7(9), the Imaj7 chord, seen in the 3rd ending, and to Fm9, the im9 chord, seen in the 4th ending. You also must negotiate a resolution to a Bmaj9 chord in the 2nd ending, which means the C7(alt.) has functioned as if it were the ♭5 substitute for G♭7(alt.). Here you should listen carefully because the #9 (D#/E♭) is sustained and simply becomes the 3rd (D#) of Bmaj7. Then there are deceptive or false cadences based upon the same kind of common tone voice-leading. For example, because we might have E♭/D# on top or within the C7(#9) voicing, that note then becomes the 9th of D♭maj9, seen in the 1st ending. That same note becomes the 5th of an A♭m9 chord, seen in the 5th ending of the chart. Finally, in the 6th ending, it becomes the major 7th of an Emaj9 chord. I felt it would make things more interesting if I sent you to these harmonic areas, and again, I feel that having eight bars of the prolonged tension is really more than enough to accomplish getting these "new" sounds in your ears and under your fingers. You might find it instructive to listen to just how I used the E♭ minor pentatonic over the C7(alt.) chord and how that same minor pentatonic then sounded beautiful over the Bmaj9 chord (there as D# minor pentatonic); over the Emaj9 chord (again as a D# minor pentatonic); and finally over the A♭m9 chord (this time played as an E♭ minor pentatonic). The E♭ minor pentatonic can simply be moved up a whole step to F minor pentatonic to resolve beautifully to the D♭maj9 chord; up a half step to E minor pentatonic to resolve to the Fmaj9 chord; and again up a simple whole step to F minor pentatonic to resolve to Fm9. Give all of these options a try when you begin your improvisations.

Another device I like very much when playing some of the pentatonics against this type of altered dominant 7th chord is to include the major 3rd as well. In my performed example, you will hear that on occasion I have used an E♮. When you are listening to the recorded example, **Track 13,** pay special attention to those eight-bar sections that precede the Bmaj7 chord (2nd ending), the Fm7 chord (4th ending), and later the Emaj7 chord (6th ending). You should also be able to hear that the E♮, that appeared prior to that last resolution was part of a G♭ dominant 7th pentatonic, and when you do this, the E♮ (F♭) is simply a built-in component of that pentatonic. Therefore, it's going to be there naturally. For me, I like it best when I can use a little cross-play between the E♭s and the E♮s since it makes the difference between the two much more pronounced. Though one almost never sees an altered dominant 7th chord for as long as eight bars, when you employ the E♮, it can sound as though you are playing the blues over this altered chordal sound. And, to my way of thinking, this is always a good thing! Give it a try when you play over **Track 14** and see what you think. Always keep in mind just where you are eventually headed for the resolution!

ALTERED DOMINANT 7TH CHORD REFERENCE CHART

CHORD	MINOR PENT. [#9]	DOM. 7th PENT. [♭5]	DOM. 7th PENT. [#5]	MINOR PENT. [7th]
C7(alt.)	E♭	G♭	A♭	B♭
D♭(alt.)	F♭	G	A	C♭
D(alt.)	F	A♭	B♭	C
E♭(alt.)	G♭	A	B	D♭
E(alt.)	G	B♭	C	D
F(alt.)	A♭	B	C#	E♭
F#(alt.)/G♭(alt.)	A/B♭♭	C	D	E/F♭
G(alt.)	B♭	D♭	E♭	F
A♭(alt.)	B/C♭	D	E	G♭
A(alt.)	C	E♭	F	G
B♭(alt.)	D♭	E	F#	A♭
B(alt.)	D	F	G	A

USING THE CD: In this case, you will hear my improvisation over the chord changes and the form from **Example 9** by playing **Track 13.** When you're ready to try to improvise over this exercise, you would simply play **Track 14.**

Example 9: Frontier Justice (Justicia de Frontera)

C7(alt.)

Mode/Scale Options:

C altered dominant/
D♭ melodic minor
(C, D♭, E♭, E, G♭, A♭, B♭)

Pentatonic Options:

E♭ minor pentatonic
(E♭, G♭, A♭, B♭, D♭)
G♭ dominant 7th pentatonic
(G♭, A♭, B♭, D♭, F♭)
A♭ dominant 7th pentatonic
(A♭, B♭, C, E♭, G♭)

1.

D♭maj7 $\binom{6}{9}$

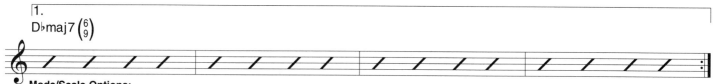

Mode/Scale Options:

D♭ major/Lydian
(D♭, E♭, F, G♭/G, A♭, B♭, C)

Pentatonic Options:

F minor pentatonic
(F, A♭, B♭, C, E♭)
C minor pentatonic
(C, E♭, F, G, B♭)
B♭ minor pentatonic
(B♭, D♭, E♭, F, A♭)

2.

B maj7 $\binom{6}{9}$

Mode/Scale Options:

B major/Lydian
(B, C♯, D♯, E/E♯, F♯, G♯, A♯)

Pentatonic Options:

D♯ minor pentatonic
(D♯, F♯, G♯, A♯, C♯)
A♯ minor pentatonic
(A♯, C♯, D♯, E♯, G♯)
G♯ minor pentatonic
(G♯, B, C♯, D♯, F♯)

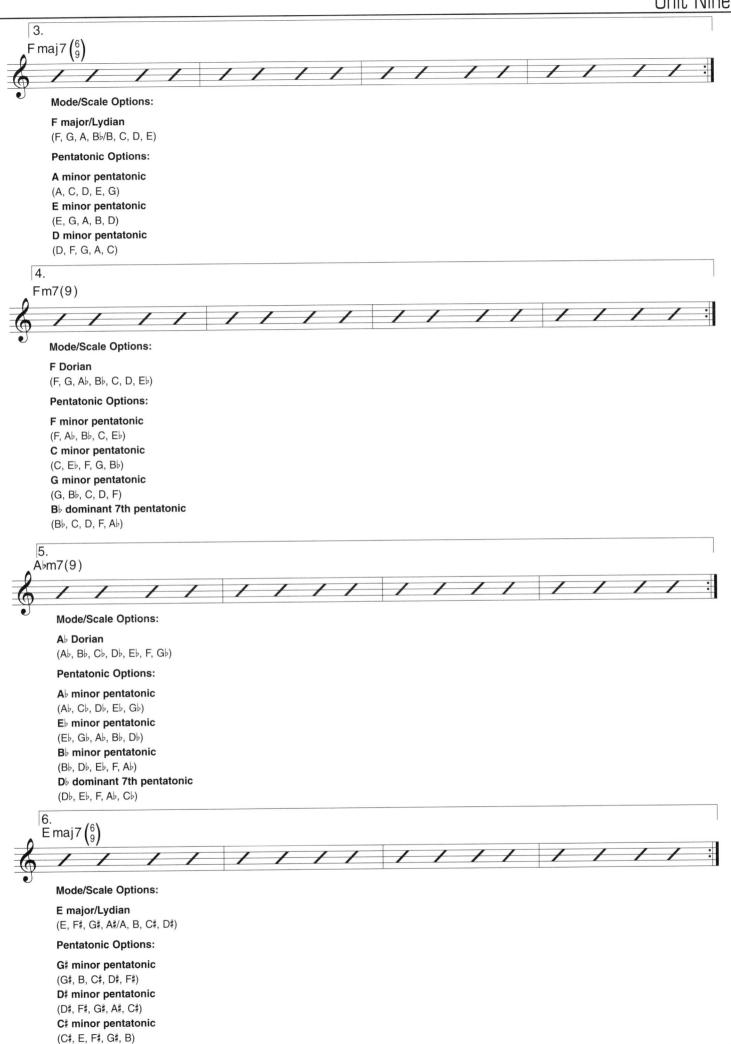

3.

F maj7 $\binom{6}{9}$

Mode/Scale Options:

F major/Lydian
(F, G, A, B♭/B, C, D, E)

Pentatonic Options:

A minor pentatonic
(A, C, D, E, G)

E minor pentatonic
(E, G, A, B, D)

D minor pentatonic
(D, F, G, A, C)

4.

Fm7(9)

Mode/Scale Options:

F Dorian
(F, G, A♭, B♭, C, D, E♭)

Pentatonic Options:

F minor pentatonic
(F, A♭, B♭, C, E♭)

C minor pentatonic
(C, E♭, F, G, B♭)

G minor pentatonic
(G, B♭, C, D, F)

B♭ dominant 7th pentatonic
(B♭, C, D, F, A♭)

5.

A♭m7(9)

Mode/Scale Options:

A♭ Dorian
(A♭, B♭, C♭, D♭, E♭, F, G♭)

Pentatonic Options:

A♭ minor pentatonic
(A♭, C♭, D♭, E♭, G♭)

E♭ minor pentatonic
(E♭, G♭, A♭, B♭, D♭)

B♭ minor pentatonic
(B♭, D♭, E♭, F, A♭)

D♭ dominant 7th pentatonic
(D♭, E♭, F, A♭, C♭)

6.

E maj7 $\binom{6}{9}$

Mode/Scale Options:

E major/Lydian
(E, F♯, G♯, A♯/A, B, C♯, D♯)

Pentatonic Options:

G♯ minor pentatonic
(G♯, B, C♯, D♯, F♯)

D♯ minor pentatonic
(D♯, F♯, G♯, A♯, C♯)

C♯ minor pentatonic
(C♯, E, F♯, G♯, B)

UNIT TEN
Pentatonic Improvising Over Cadences —————————————————————

Pentatonic Improvising for iim7–V7(alt.)–Imaj7–[VI7(alt.)]

For those of you most interested in applying these concepts to jazz and jazz-related music, there can be little doubt that learning to negotiate cadences to both major and minor chords will serve as the best proof of the usefulness of pentatonics in "real" music. By "real" music, or "real" tunes, I am referring to standards both from the world of popular music and the jazz world as well. I've presented the examples so that they function within the same key (Bb) since Bb major and G minor are relatives of one another and have the same key signatures. I have gone to great lengths to present these materials so that, at least in this key, all of your options appear right before you.

First you are given the chord progression as it appears on the play-along CD. Below the progression, each of the chords within its chord family is presented in its own compartment. Below the chord name, I have attempted to remind you of the "formula" for which the minor and dominant 7th pentatonics could be applied within each chord family. Then, below that, each possibility is provided in detail. The notes that sound within each minor and dominant 7th pentatonic are given, and just above them is the scale degree they would produce relative to the root of the chord. If you recall, in earlier chapters I tried to present my personal choices for the best sounding pentatonics per chord family with some allowances for the style of music. As a reminder of the pentatonics that I felt contained a questionable note, I have placed that scale degree within brackets ([ ]). It is my hope that if something did sound strange to your ears, that these bracketed notes might help explain that feeling. Then, in the end, you would have to decide if that particular pentatonic is ever appropriate for your use—the way you hear things!

There is a sense to this kind of presentation that you could mix-and-match your options, choosing one box in a column and then jumping over to any box in the next column. There would be nothing wrong with such an approach, because in the end your ear would be the best judge of what is musical and effective. If you try this out, and I think you should, try to finger each pentatonic in the same position, or as close to it as you can construct it. If this causes difficulty when playing along with the CD, then try to break it down, fingering the pentatonics as slowly as needed until you have created a sense of melodic flow.

How many times have you listened to one of your favorite improvisers and heard them play a motif (a phrase, a lick, etc.) and then they seem to play it up or down a half step? Was that just a device, something they learned from a record or from a friend? Or is it possible that a logical harmonic principle was being employed? Well, probably all of these cases are true in degrees, but I would like to believe that you'll come to feel as I do that the latter is really the case. There are sound harmonic principles at play when this device is employed properly. If you can understand this and see that there is an almost mathematical logic at play, then learn to employ the concept over cadences to major and minor chords—it will broaden your approach to playing on standards as well as your freer playing over pedals and vamps. Let's take a look at some of the concepts that could be applied.

To illustrate this point, I have a particular favorite pentatonic strategy that is drawn directly from the boxes. I've used this one example in my private teaching as well as at all of my clinics, seminars, and master classes. It involves, in my opinion, the most colorful options over each of the three chords. I chose G minor pentatonic (the minor pentatonic built from the 5th) to play over the Cm7 chord; Ab minor pentatonic (the minor pentatonic built upon the #9 to play over the F7(alt.) chord; and A minor pentatonic (the minor pentatonic built from the major 7th) to play over the Bbmaj7 chord. So, if you break down the movement, you are going from G minor pentatonic up one half step to Ab minor pentatonic and then up one half step to an A minor pentatonic. If this progression was to loop itself around again by adding a VI7(alt.) chord (that being G7[alt.] in this key), then you would simply go up yet another half step, applying Bb minor pentatonic. So, you have just gone up with parallel minor pentatonics and still played through what has to be considered the most basic and important progression in Western music. For some, this can be the most difficult hurdle to cross when learning to play through changes.

Even if you chose not to play through the written examples, try using the G minor pentatonic fingering that feels the most comfortable for you, and play something, anything, you hear over the Cm7 chord; then move what you just played up by one half step for the F7(alt.); and finally up one more half step for the B♭maj7 chord too. Listen to what that sounds like over the recorded play-along example. Then, change your phrasing and keep experimenting with different configurations of the notes **and** the usage of the other four fingerings for the guitar. I've tried to give my written examples simplicity while still offering a sense of the development of an idea through the changes.

Give the examples a try and then map out some pentatonic choices from the boxes that look like they'd sound good, ones that might not present tricky fingering problems at the outset. Perhaps try listening to D minor pentatonic over the Cm7 chord, E♭ pentatonic over the F7(alt.) [just be careful with the B♭], and then back down a half step to the D minor pentatonic, this time over B♭maj7. All you've had to do is go up one half step and then back down one half step. It looks simple enough on paper, but **how does it sound to you?**

I encourage you not to shy away from the use of the dominant 7th pentatonic just because right now it might be the least familiar to you. Please force yourself to work it into your practice and experimentation regimen. In trying to offer some examples that keep the letter names of the pentatonics as close as a half step as possible, try playing D minor pentatonic over the Cm7 chord, then D♭ dominant 7th pentatonic over the F7(alt.) chord, and then D minor pentatonic over the B♭maj7 chord. Once you've decided that this offers a good sound and interesting linear shapes, try starting the D minor pentatonic in each of the five basic fingering positions and then move them over to the closest and most logical fingering for the D♭ dominant 7th pentatonic scale. With a lot of concentrated work spent on this aspect, it should be a far less frightening prospect to use the once foreign dominant 7th pentatonic.

When I was introducing the origins of the minor pentatonic, I pointed out that some of you might have already learned this but thought of it as the relative major pentatonic (R, 2nd, 3rd, 5th, and 6th). If you have retained this orientation, you can still apply it and create some other linear relationships with great proximity. For example, if you were to think of G minor pentatonic as its relative major, B♭ major pentatonic, and then play that over the Cm7 chord, as you moved to negotiate the F7(alt.) chord using the B-dominant 7th pentatonic, you would see that you are only going up by one half step again. Give it a try. How about thinking of C minor pentatonic as its relative major, E♭ major pentatonic, and then playing it over the Cm7 chord? Then, as the F7(alt.) chord arrived, you could simply try playing the E♭ minor pentatonic. Here you've just gone from the major pentatonic to the minor pentatonic of the same tonal center. Sounds easy—now see how it sounds! Perhaps it won't sound as good as it looks to be easy.

Before we continue and discuss the options for cadences resolving to a minor chord (im7), you must always remember that **virtually all options are possible on a V7(alt.) chord** when it resolves to a major chord (Imaj7). Those options could be: **[1]** the altered dominant scale, which has the same notes as **[2]** the Super Locrian mode and also the same notes as **[3]** the melodic minor scale one half step above the root; **[4]** the diminished scale: half step and whole step alternating from the root; **[5]** the whole-tone scale; **[6]** the Dorian mode built upon the 7th degree of the V7 chord producing a Phrygian sound; **[7]** and it's also possible to just play the major scale of the Imaj7 chord through everything if you avoid playing the major 7th degree over the VI7(alt.) chord. In this key, B♭, you should avoid playing A♮ over the G7(alt.) chord. A pentatonic option that accomplishes this same thing, in a more bluesy fashion, is done by simply using the G minor pentatonic over the entire progression. Try it and see how it sounds!

I also hasten to add that being able to play through cadences using these techniques and disciplines will not necessarily make you a great jazz player. Jazz-oriented lines through cadences have their own shapes and linear melodic configurations. Again, like any other musical style or genre, jazz has its own language, and to really make something sound like jazz, you must speak the language properly. Essentially, that language has developed in the twentieth century, and most of it, as it has been passed along, comes from the big band era and later the smaller bebop and hard bop groups that came on strong during the late

'40s and '50s, and which continue to this day.

If you are already a fluent jazz player, these pentatonic systems will, without question, add an angular quality to your lines, and they will help remove some traces of the scale-oriented quality to those same lines if that is one of your major self-criticisms. If you come from a rock, blues, or jazz-rock fusion background and have a deep desire to feel more at ease in handling these kinds of progressions without sounding too jazzy, then these concepts should keep you close enough to your rock and blues roots while supplying the tools for playing over more sophisticated chord changes.

Beyond the recorded examples presented in this book, if you would like to listen to an extended improvisation using these pentatonics over the double-time feel **(Example 10-J),** then you would first go to **Track 15** from CD #2, the **RED CD,** in **CONTEMPORARY CHORD KHANCEPTS.** This particular improvisation, over a classic turnaround, also represents how I approach creating tension and release by venturing outside the more consonant aspects of the chord changes. Because the texture is so open (remember there is only a bass and percussion accompaniment), don't be fooled by some of the lines, which might seem to be "out" sounding. Many such lines are actually just those that have become perfectly normal to my ears when creating cadences from any altered dominant 7th to both major and minor chords. However, everything, "in" or "out," is done with a linear purpose as the lines seek a graceful resolution. The fundamentals of this approach to improvising are addressed in great detail in **Unit 13** of this publication. What I improvised on the aforementioned **Track 15** became the shell for my tune, "Charanga Sí Sí." which was later recorded by the **Caribbean Jazz Project** on **NEW HORIZONS** (Concord Picante). The complete lead sheets can be accessed by visiting the **KHAN'S KORNER 2** page at **www.stevekhan.com/korner2.htm.**

PENTATONIC IMPROVISING FOR: iim7 – V7(alt.) – Imaj7 – [VI7(alt.)]

Cm7	F7(alt.)	B♭maj7	G7(alt.)
use minor pentatonic built from Root, 2nd, and 5th and the dominant 7th pentatonic built from the 4th	use minor pentatonic built from #9 and dominant 7th pentatonic built from ♭5 and #5	use minor pentatonic built from 3rd, maj7th, and 6th	use minor pentatonic built from #9 and dominant 7th pentatonics built from ♭5 and #5
C minor pent. R m3rd 4th 5th 7th **C E♭ F G B♭**	**A♭ minor pent.** #9 ♭5 #5 7th ♭9 **A♭ C♭ D♭ E♭ G♭**	**D minor pent.** 3rd 5th 6th maj7 9th **D F G A C**	**B♭ minor pent.** #9 ♭5 #5 7th ♭9 **B♭ D♭ E♭ F A♭**
D minor pent. 9th 4th 5th 6th R **D F G A C**	**B dom. 7th pent.** ♭5 #5 7th ♭9 3rd **B C# D# F# A**	**A minor pent.** maj7 9th 3rd #4 6th **A C D E G**	**D♭ dom. 7th pent.** ♭5 #5 7th ♭9 3rd **D♭ E♭ F A♭ C♭**
G minor pent. 5th 7th R 9th 4th **G B♭ C D F**	**D♭ dom. 7th pent.** #5 7th R #9 ♭5 **D♭ E♭ F A♭ C♭**	**G minor pent.** 6th [R] 9th 3rd 5th **G B♭ C D F**	**E♭ dom. 7th pent.** #5 7th R #9 ♭5 **E♭ F G B♭ D♭**
F dom. 7th pent. 4th 5th 6th R m3rd **F G A C E♭**			

Example 10: Pentatonic iim-V-I Examples

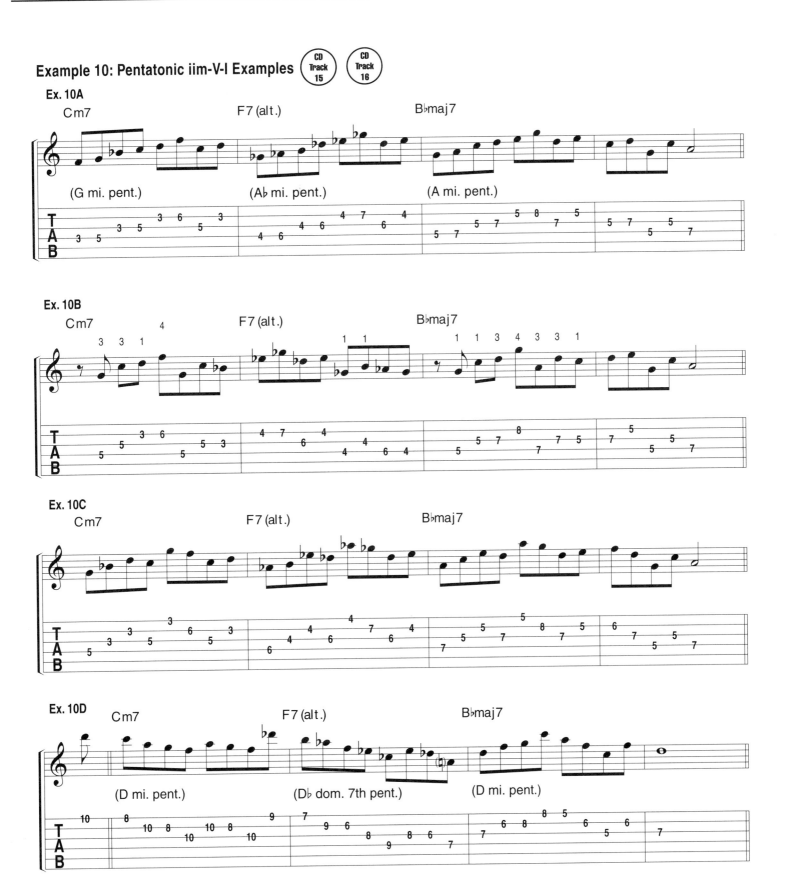

Ex. 10E

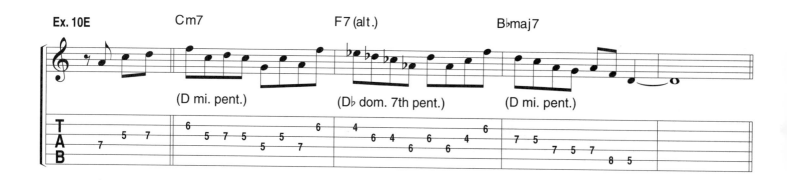

Ex. 10F

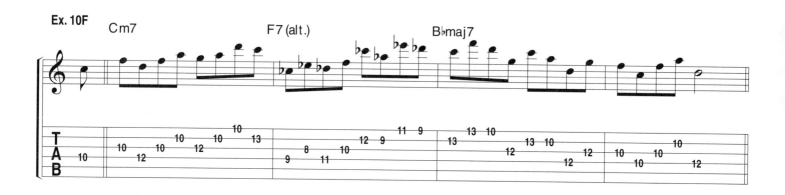

Ex. 10G

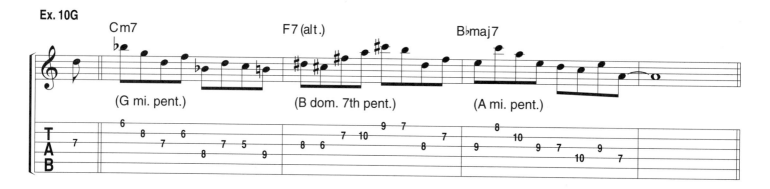

Ex. 10H

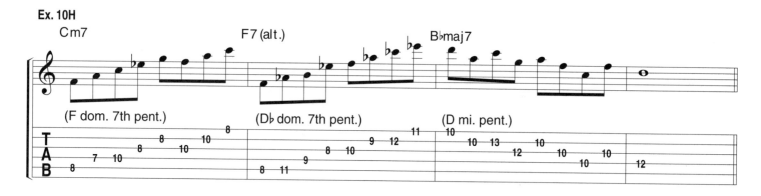

USING THE CD: To hear **Examples 10A–10D** performed, play **Track 15.** What you will hear is that each example, a four-bar phrase, is performed twice before I moved on to the next one. When you feel ready to try playing along with the examples yourself or just want to improvise using these new concepts, play along with **Track 16.** If you are ready to improvise over the full chord progression that adds the VI7(alt.) chord, then use **Track 21,** which is now titled, "Sol Motion." "Charanga C.C." presents the same harmonic challenges only in double-time. To improvise over this, use **Track 22.**

Example 10I: Sol Motion [ii-V7(alt.)-I-VI7(alt.)]

CD Track 21

Cm7   F7   F7 (alt.)   Bbmaj7   G7 (alt.)

Mode/Scale Options:

C Dorian/F Mixolydian
(C, D, Eb, F, G, A, Bb)

Pentatonic Options:

G minor pentatonic
(G, Bb, C, D, F)
C minor pentatonic
(C, Eb, F, G, Bb)
D minor pentatonic
(D, F, G, A, C)
F dominant 7th pentatonic
(F, G, A, C, Eb)

Mode/Scale Options:

**F altered dominant/
Gb melodic minor**
(F, Gb, Ab, A, B/Cb, C#/Db, Eb)
**F half-tone/whole-tone
diminished scale**
(F, Gb, Ab, A, B, C, D, Eb)
F whole-tone scale
(F, G, A, B, C#, Eb)

Pentatonic Options:

Ab minor pentatonic
(Ab, Cb, Db, Eb, Gb)
B dominant 7th pentatonic
(B, C#, D#, F#, A)
Db dominant 7th pentatonic
(Db, Eb, F, Ab, Cb)

Mode/Scale Options:

Bb major/Lydian
(Bb, C, D, Eb/E, F, G, A)

Pentatonic Options:

D minor pentatonic
(D, F, G, A, C)
A minor pentatonic
(A, C, D, E, G)
G minor pentatonic
(G, Bb, C, D, F)

Mode/Scale Options:

**G altered dominant/
Ab melodic minor**
(G, Ab, Bb, B, Db, Eb, F)
C harmonic minor
(C, D, Eb, F, G, Ab, B)

Pentatonic Options:

Bb minor pentatonic
(Bb, Db, Eb, F, Ab)
Db dominant 7th pentatonic
(Db, Eb, F, Ab, Cb)
Eb dominant 7th pentatonic
(Eb, F, G, Bb, Db)

Example 10J: Charanga C.C. [ii-V7(alt.)-I-VI7(alt.)]

CD Track 22

Cm7   F7   F7 (alt.)

Mode/Scale Options:

C Dorian/F Mixolydian
(C, D, Eb, F, G, A, Bb)

Pentatonic Options:

G minor pentatonic
(G, Bb, C, D, F)
C minor pentatonic
(C, Eb, F, G, Bb)
D minor pentatonic
(D, F, G, A, C)
F dominant 7th pentatonic
(F, G, A, C, Eb)

Mode/Scale Options:

**F altered dominant/
Gb melodic minor**
(F, Gb, Ab, A, B/Cb, C#/Db, Eb)
**F half-tone/whole-tone
diminished scale**
(F, Gb, Ab, A, B, C, D, Eb)
F whole-tone scale
(F, G, A, B, C#, Eb)

Pentatonic Options:

Ab minor pentatonic
(Ab, Cb, Db, Eb, Gb)
B dominant 7th pentatonic
(B, C#, D#, F#, A)
Db dominant 7th pentatonic
(Db, Eb, F, Ab, Cb)

Bbmaj7   G7 (alt.)

Mode/Scale Options:

Bb major/Lydian
(Bb, C, D, Eb/E, F, G, A)

Pentatonic Options:

D minor pentatonic
(D, F, G, A, C)
A minor pentatonic
(A, C, D, E, G)
G minor pentatonic
(G, Bb, C, D, F)

Mode/Scale Options:

**G altered dominant/
Ab melodic minor**
(G, Ab, Bb, B, Db, Eb, F)
C harmonic minor
(C, D, Eb, F, G, Ab, B)

Pentatonic Options:

Bb minor pentatonic
(Bb, Db, Eb, F, Ab)
Db dominant 7th pentatonic
(Db, Eb, F, Ab, Cb)
Eb dominant 7th pentatonic
(Eb, F, G, Bb, Db)

UNIT ELEVEN
Pentatonic Improvising iim7(♭5)–V7(alt.)–im7

As I tried to point out in the prior chapter, you can use all of your scale options when negotiating a cadence to a major chord. However, when the resolution of the cadence is to a minor chord, some of these options are just not going to sound as good. With this in mind, your options might now be the following:

[1] the altered dominant scale, which has the same notes as:

[2] the Super Locrian mode, still the same notes as:

[3] the melodic minor scale one half step above the root;

[4] the harmonic minor scale of the im7 chord;

[5] the Dorian mode built from the 7th degree of the V7(alt.) chord.

The reason I would not recommend playing the diminshed scale over a V7 (alt.) chord that is headed towards a im7 is that, on its 7th degree, it is producing the natural 13th (6th degree), which could rub against the ♭5 or ♯5 were they to be used by an accompanist, but that note is also what would be the major 3rd of the next chord you are moving toward and that chord is a minor chord! So, you would have to be very careful in using the diminished scale. The use of the whole-tone scale presents other problems since its 2nd degree is the natural 9th, which could rub against the ♭9 or ♯9 if they were present in the V7(alt.) chord structure. Again, you would have to exercise great care. Though I've mentioned this in the earlier section dealing with the m7(♭5) chord family, it bears repeating that you can play blues-based material built from the root of the im7 chord through the entire iim7(♭5)–V7(alt.)–im7 progression. In the example, you would just play G blues lines across the entire progression.

Here's my suggestion for the best place to start when committing yourself to the discipline of using only pentatonics while playing through these cadences. Keep in mind that when you are really playing with other musicians, you would probably not play something so regimented and would be using all of your linear options. Those options, in the end, should be solely based upon what you really hear! To negotiate the m7(♭5)–V7(alt.) chords, I would always begin by using the two best sounding or can't-miss pentatonic choices! For the m7(♭5), I would start by using the minor pentatonic built from the m3rd, and for the V7(alt.) chord I would use the minor pentatonic built from the ♯9. In the example, using the key of G minor, try using C minor pentatonic over the Am7(♭5) chord and F minor pentatonic over the D7(alt.) chord. As you arrive at the im7 chord, all of the options will sound good, so try to choose one that happens to finger nearest to where you are on the fingerboard. The more you put this to use, the more the fingerboard of the guitar will begin to look much more like what the keyboard looks like to a pianist. The result is that your playing will take on a greater economy of movement and your improvisations will be much more efficient and therefore **more melodic.** Again, take some chances by forcing yourself to put the dominant 7th pentatonic to use whenever you can because it will add much more color to your solos.

Though **Track 17** provides you with the chance to play over the basic iim7(♭5)–V7(alt.)–im7 progression, I also provided one example which adds some variety and helps turn around this simple cadence. You can view these extended cadences in **Example 12** where it becomes a little 16-bar tune, which I have titled "Clare as Day." In the fourth bar of each four-bar phrase, I have given you a slightly different challenge. In bar 4, we begin by staying on our im7 chord. In bar 8, we go up to a B♭m7–E♭7 movement. To negotiate this change, simply begin by trying to use B♭ minor pentatonic, or F minor pentatonic, always two of your easiest and best options. Then, in **bar 12,** you are given a C7(9) chord, and though the bass note is changing, you are really remaining in the same mode, G Dorian. That is to say, you don't have to change anything you are doing even though the chord is "changing" below. Finally, in **bars 15–16,** you see that you are given, for two beats each, Gm7–C7 for a bar and then Fm7–B♭7 for a bar. During that last bar, simply try to use F minor pentatonic or C minor pentatonic and see how those sounds work. The great thing about using the C minor pentatonic is that it can be continued right into **bar 1** of the progression over the Am7(♭5) chord because it is your best sounding option! This, of course, gives the potential for great melodic continuity.

PENTATONIC IMPROVISING FOR: iim7(♭5)–V7(alt.)–im7

Am7(♭5)	D7(alt.)	Gm7	[Optional Changes]
use minor pentatonics built from m3rd, 4th, 7th; and the dominant 7th pentatonic built from the 6th	use minor pentatonic built from #9; and the dominant 7th pentatonics built from ♭5 and #5	use minor pentatonics built from Root, 2nd, and 5th; and the dominant 7th pentatonic built from the 4th	B♭m7–E♭7 C7(9) Fm7–B♭7
C minor pent. m3rd ♭5 6th 7th 9th C E♭ F G B♭	**F minor pent.** #9 ♭5 #5 7th ♭9 F A♭ B♭ C E♭	**G minor pent.** R m3rd 4th 5th 7th G B♭ C D F	
D minor pent. 4th 6th 7th Fm 3rd D F G A C	**A♭ dom. 7th pent.** ♭5 #5 7th ♭9 3rd A♭ B♭ C E♭ G♭	**A minor pent.** 9th 4th 5th 6th R A C D E G	
G minor pent. 7th 9th m3rd 4th 6th G B♭ C D F	**B♭ dom. 7th pent.** #5 7th R #9 ♭5 B♭ C D F A♭	**D minor pent.** 5th 7th R 9th 4th D F G A C	
F dom. 7th pent. 6th 7th R m3rd ♭5 F G A C E♭		**C dom. 7th pent.** 4th 5th 6th Rm 3rd C D E G B♭	

USING THE CD: To hear **Examples 11A–D** performed, play **Track 17.** What you will again hear is that each example, a four-bar phrase, is performed twice before I moved on to the next one. When you feel ready to try playing these examples yourself or just want to improvise using these new concepts, play along with **Track 18.** To hear my improvised piece over the changes you've been provided with in **Example 12,** play **Track 19.** To practice improvising over these changes, use the **Track 20** play-along.

Original pen and ink by Jean-Michel Folon. Given to Steve as a gift for a possible songbook cover in 1980.
This drawing is reminiscent of Folon's painting for the cover of *The Blue Man* LP from '78.

Example 11: Pentatonic iim7(♭5)–V–im Examples (in Gm)

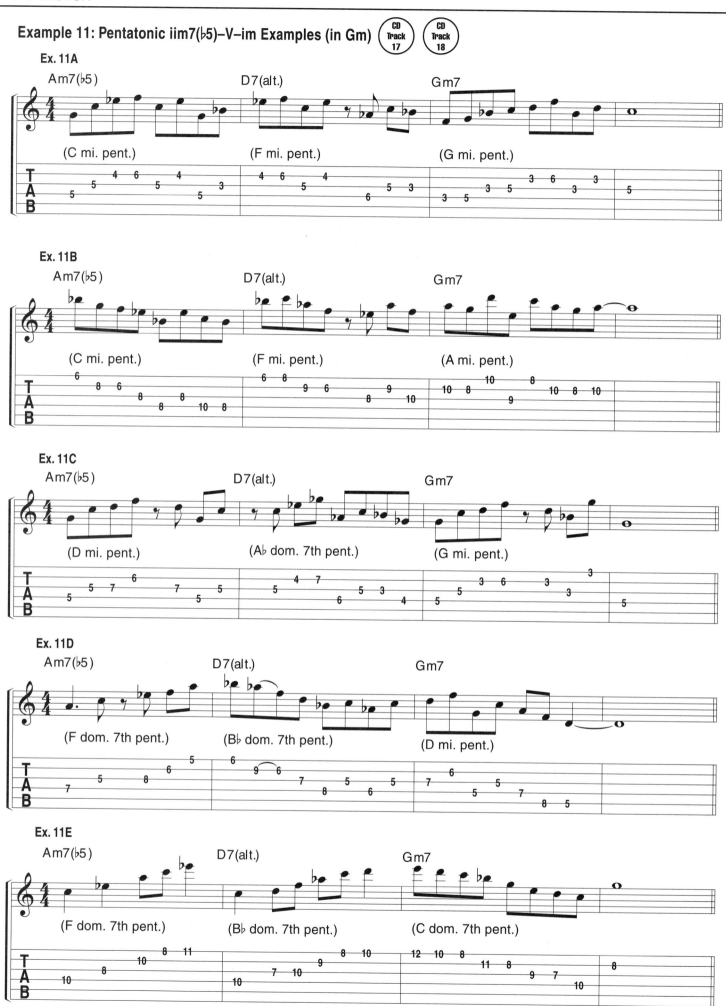

Steve Khan

Example 12: Clare as Day [iim7(♭5)–V–i (in Gm)]

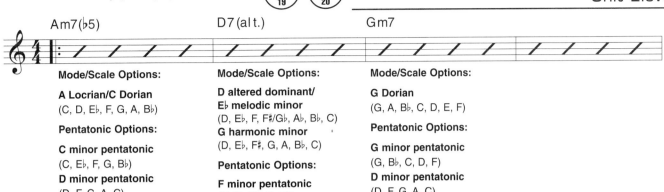

Am7(♭5) ― **D7(alt.)** ― **Gm7**

Mode/Scale Options:

A Locrian/C Dorian
(C, D, E♭, F, G, A, B♭)

Pentatonic Options:

C minor pentatonic
(C, E♭, F, G, B♭)
D minor pentatonic
(D, F, G, A, C)
G minor pentatonic
(G, B♭, C, D, F)
F dominant 7th pentatonic
(F, G, A, C, E♭)

Mode/Scale Options:

**D altered dominant/
E♭ melodic minor**
(D, E♭, F, F♯/G♭, A♭, B♭, C)
G harmonic minor
(D, E♭, F♯, G, A, B♭, C)

Pentatonic Options:

F minor pentatonic
(F, A♭, B♭, C, E♭)
A♭ dominant 7th pentatonic
(A♭, B♭, C, E♭, G♭)
B♭ dominant 7th pentatonic
(B♭, C, D, F, A♭)

Mode/Scale Options:

G Dorian
(G, A, B♭, C, D, E, F)

Pentatonic Options:

G minor pentatonic
(G, B♭, C, D, F)
D minor pentatonic
(D, F, G, A, C)
A minor pentatonic
(A, C, D, E, G)
C dominant 7th pentatonic
(C, D, E, G, B♭)

Am7(♭5) ― **D7(alt.)** ― **Gm7** ― **B♭m7** ― **E♭7**

Mode/Scale Options:

A Locrian/C Dorian
(C, D, E♭, F, G, A, B♭)

Pentatonic Options:

C minor pentatonic
(C, E♭, F, G, B♭)
D minor pentatonic
(D, F, G, A, C)
G minor pentatonic
(G, B♭, C, D, F)
F dominant 7th pentatonic
(F, G, A, C, E♭)

Mode/Scale Options:

**D altered dominant/
E♭ melodic minor**
(D, E♭, F, F♯/G♭, A♭, B♭, C)
G harmonic minor
(D, E♭, F♯, G, A, B♭, C)

Pentatonic Options:

F minor pentatonic
(F, A♭, B♭, C, E♭)
A♭ dominant 7th pentatonic
(A♭, B♭, C, E♭, G♭)
B♭ dominant 7th pentatonic
(B♭, C, D, F, A♭)

Mode/Scale Options:

G Dorian
(G, A, B♭, C, D, E, F)

Pentatonic Options:

G minor pentatonic
(G, B♭, C, D, F)
D minor pentatonic
(D, F, G, A, C)
A minor pentatonic
(A, C, D, E, G)
C dominant 7th pentatonic
(C, D, E, G, B♭)

Mode/Scale Options:

B♭ Dorian
(B♭, C, D♭, E♭, F, G, A♭)

Pentatonic Options:

B♭ minor pentatonic
(B♭, D♭, E♭, F, A♭)
F minor pentatonic
(F, A♭, B♭, C, E♭)
C minor pentatonic
(C, E♭, F, G, B♭)
E♭ dominant 7th pentatonic
(E♭, F, G, B♭, D♭)

Am7(♭5) ― **D7(alt.)** ― **Gm7** ― **C7**

Mode/Scale Options:

A Locrian/C Dorian
(C, D, E♭, F, G, A, B♭)

Pentatonic Options:

C minor pentatonic
(C, E♭, F, G, B♭)
D minor pentatonic
(D, F, G, A, C)
G minor pentatonic
(G, B♭, C, D, F)
F dominant 7th pentatonic
(F, G, A, C, E♭)

Mode/Scale Options:

**D altered dominant/
E♭ melodic minor**
(D, E♭, F, F♯/G♭, A♭, B♭, C)
G harmonic minor
(D, E♭, F♯, G, A, B♭, C)

Pentatonic Options:

F minor pentatonic
(F, A♭, B♭, C, E♭)
A♭ dominant 7th pentatonic
(A♭, B♭, C, E♭, G♭)
B♭ dominant 7th pentatonic
(B♭, C, D, F, A♭)

Mode/Scale Options:

G Dorian
(G, A, B♭, C, D, E, F)

Pentatonic Options:

G minor pentatonic
(G, B♭, C, D, F)
D minor pentatonic
(D, F, G, A, C)
A minor pentatonic
(A, C, D, E, G)
C dominant 7th pentatonic
(C, D, E, G, B♭)

Am7(♭5) ― **D7(alt.)** ― **Gm7** ― **C7** ― **Fm7** ― **B♭7**

Mode/Scale Options:

A Locrian/C Dorian
(C, D, E♭, F, G, A, B♭)

Pentatonic Options:

C minor pentatonic
(C, E♭, F, G, B♭)
D minor pentatonic
(D, F, G, A, C)
G minor pentatonic
(G, B♭, C, D, F)
F dominant 7th pentatonic
(F, G, A, C, E♭)

Mode/Scale Options:

**D altered dominant/
E♭ melodic minor**
(D, E♭, F, F♯/G♭, A♭, B♭, C)
G harmonic minor
(D, E♭, F♯, G, A, B♭, C)

Pentatonic Options:

F minor pentatonic
(F, A♭, B♭, C, E♭)
A♭ dominant 7th pentatonic
(A♭, B♭, C, E♭, G♭)
B♭ dominant 7th pentatonic
(B♭, C, D, F, A♭)

Mode/Scale Options:

G Dorian
(G, A, B♭, C, D, E, F)

Pentatonic Options:

G minor pentatonic
(G, B♭, C, D, F)
D minor pentatonic
(D, F, G, A, C)
A minor pentatonic
(A, C, D, E, G)
C dominant 7th pentatonic
(C, D, E, G, B♭)

Mode/Scale Options:

F Dorian
(F, G, A♭, B♭, C, D, E♭)

Pentatonic Options:

F minor pentatonic
(F, A♭, B♭, C, E♭)
C minor pentatonic
(C, E♭, F, G, B♭)
G minor pentatonic
(G, B♭, C, D, F)
B♭ dominant 7th pentatonic
(B♭, C, D, F, A♭)

UNIT TWELVE
Pentatonics in Sequence Exercises ———————————————

One of the most important, useful, and musical devices in developing your improvisational skills is taking an idea and expanding upon it for what could be a brief time or what might even become the "theme" of an entire solo on any given night. The following series of exercises, which appear over cadences to both major and minor, are presented in the form of sequential musical ideas that move through the changes while traveling up the fingerboard. Notice that the first examples use the three ascending minor pentatonics. In **Examples 13F–J** and **14B–D,** I have attempted to force you to use the dominant 7th pentatonic so that it will become less and less of a stranger.

For the examples offered over the iim7(♭5)–V7(alt.)–im7 progression, I've taken a different rhythmic approach and put into use sixteenth-note subdivisions. Like the eighth-note ideas presented, you can see that the sequence is as much a rhythmic sequence as it is a pitch-oriented one.

USING THE CD: **Track 15** begins with **Examples 10A–D.** To hear **Examples 13A–D,** go past **Examples 10A–D** (1:04 into the track); you will hear a four-bar vamp followed by **Examples 13A–D** (**Examples 13E–J** are not included on the recording). Again, you will hear that each four-bar example was performed twice before I moved on to the next one. When you feel ready to try playing the examples yourself or just want to improvise using these new concepts, play along with **Track 16.**

Example 13: Pentatonic Sequences (ii–V–I)

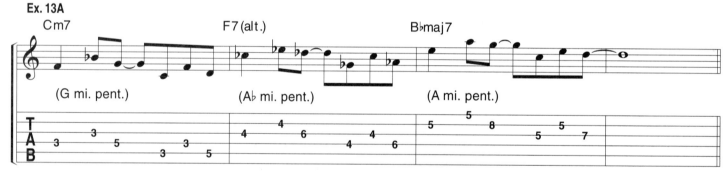

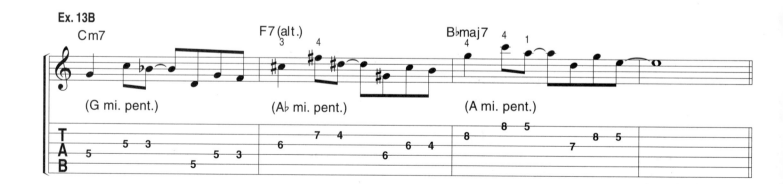

Ex. 13C

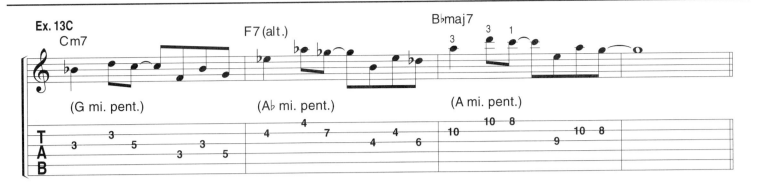

Ex. 13D

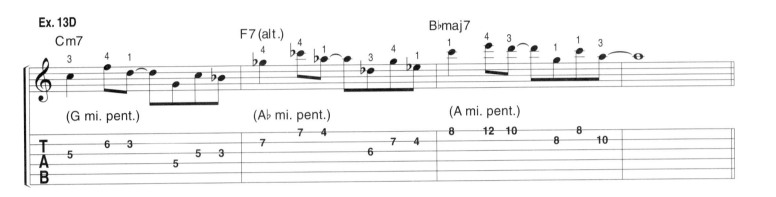

Ex. 13E

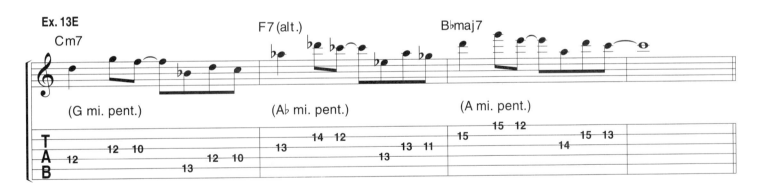

Ex. 13F

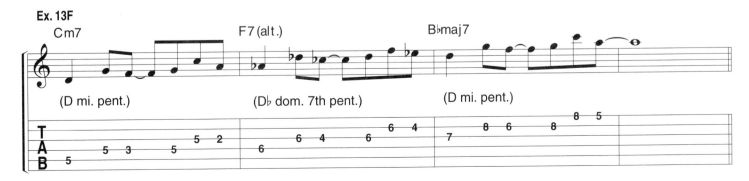

Unit Twelve

Ex. 13G

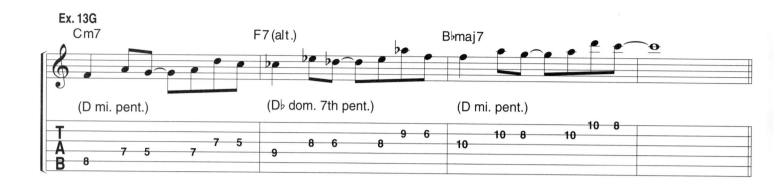

Ex. 13H

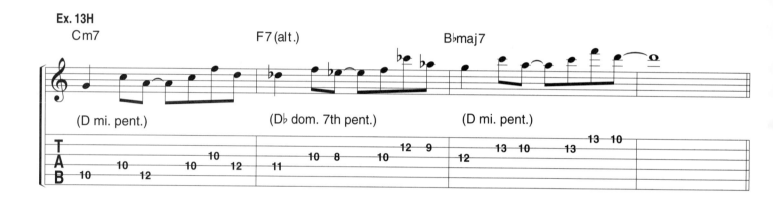

Ex. 13I

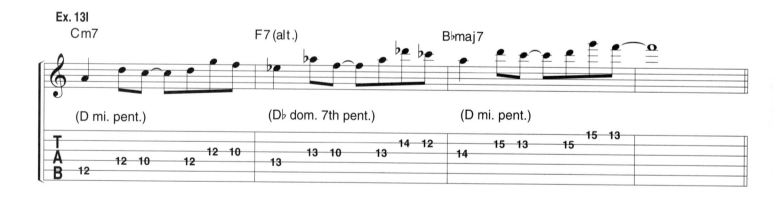

Ex. 13J

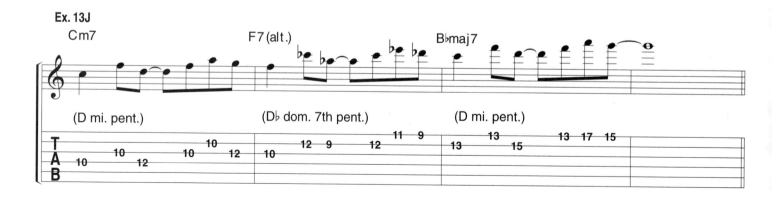

USING THE CD: Track 17 begins with **Examples 11A–D.** To hear **Examples 14A–14D** go past **Examples 11A–D** (1:04 into the track), you will hear a four-bar vamp followed by **Examples 14A–D.** When you feel ready to try playing the examples yourself, or just want to improvise using these new concepts, play along with **Track 18.**

Example 14: Pentatonic Sequences (iim7♭5–V–i)

UNIT THIRTEEN
Pentatonics Around and Outside the Consonant

Though the prior book is devoted to chords, somewhere toward the end of that spectrum should be a sensibility about those chords and the part they play when lines reach outside the traditional boundaries of scales and modes. In this one section dedicated to the shape of your lines, I offer my analysis for venturing beyond the traditional—the consonant—when approaching any of the three main chord families: dominant, minor, and major. This topic could certainly be the work of another book entirely. However, since I am often asked about this, and since the pentatonics can play such an important role, I wanted to include a discussion of the topic in this book. I have decided to confine this discussion, however, to only the dominant 7th chord family. My hope is that the suggestions derived from my work will give you the courage to explore these harmonic concepts.

For the purpose of this study, we will begin by using G7 as our center, our home base so to speak. Taken at face value, the mode most likely to be associated with dominant 7th chords treated diatonically is the Mixolydian mode; its seven notes in this key area would be G, A, B, C, D, E, and F. As it's known and commonly accepted, there are only twelve tones in our well-tempered system. Since the mode gives us seven of those pitches within the harmony, we are left with just five more tones to examine. If you were to add into this mix the language of the blues, our common ground, we could add the blue notes: ♯2nd or ♭3rd and the ♭5. In the area of the G7, our example tonal center, we would be speaking of B♭ and D♭. So, with this notion accepted, we have now used nine of the twelve tones.

What now remains would be the A♭ (the ♭9); D♯ (the ♯5); and F♯ (the maj7th). In the world of jazz, the sounds of the ♭9 and the ♯5 are not all that foreign to our ears. In the popular music of the post-Beatles era, such sounds are readily found in the music of artists like Steely Dan, Sting, and many others too numerous to mention. So, could these pitches really be that out or that wrong? Only the maj7th (F♯) seems to be out of place here.

Perhaps what makes something sound outside would be the grouping of the notes in a phrase more than any one isolated pitch. I believe that the concept should never be about playing something so outrageous that you draw too much attention to it. Whatever you play should function within the natural flow of your improvisation and the music as a whole. Sometimes making too much of one dissonant note can really be heard and felt as just plain irritating more than being "far out" or even interesting sounding. During what I suppose could be called their great middle years of recording, the mid-'60s, Miles Davis (Columbia/Sony Music) and John Coltrane (Impulse!) improvised, at times, over one isolated chord change. If you go back to these recordings and, while you're listening, analyze the tonal centers and chord family; then, when you hear any pitch/note to which you have an emotional response, stop the recording, locate that note, and see how it does or does not fit within the framework of your initial modal analysis. Once you have labeled its scale degree relative to the root, try to transcribe the few pitches that precede or follow it. These pitches together might suggest a thought or harmonic process being employed by one of these great masters. This just might give you a key to what kind of notes/pitches and lines **you** hear.

In any profession, your **imagination** is of vital importance. Let's accept, for the purpose of this discussion, that much of the outside harmonic world has some kind of dominant function because we are trying to create the tension that must be released. Then with the dominant 7th chord family, we might imagine that, over a pedal (in this case a G pedal), we could create tension by introducing the V7(alt.) chord sounds of D7(alt.). In the diagram, outside our home base box, I have written out all the possible D7 alterations for the creation of this tension.

Basically, all of these options can, in part, be derived from the altered dominant scale (Super Locrian mode or melodic minor scale a half step above the root of the dominant). In our example here, that would be the E♭ melodic minor (E♭, F, G♭, A♭, B♭, C, and D). In any case, the seven tones are exactly the same, just at times enharmonically spelled.

From my listening, especially to Coltrane and McCoy Tyner, our same two basic pentatonic scale formations were vital to their work of that period—the minor pentatonic (Root, m3rd, 4th, 5th, ♭7th) and what I've come to label as the dominant 7th pentatonic (Root, 2nd, 3rd, 5th, ♭7th). My own formulas for creating the altered sounds, using these two pentatonic formations, would be to apply minor pentatonics built from the ♯9 and the 7th degrees and the dominant 7th pentatonics built from the ♭5 and ♯5. So, relative to D as our root, we could apply F minor pentatonic (the ♯9); C minor pentatonic (the 7th); A♭ dominant 7th pentatonic (the ♭5); and B♭ dominant 7th pentatonic (the ♯5).

Following the lines on the provided chart, **Example 15,** you can see that, in some cases, I have simply extended these pentatonic groupings into their fully realized seven-tone modes. F minor pentatonic has become F Dorian, and C minor pentatonic has become C Dorian. How do you best venture into this area without feeling as though you are forcing something to happen? Perhaps you are trying to make something happen that is just not ready to happen? Again, a simple concept works best. I suggest using the common tones as a **musical window** from which to enter this outer harmonic world. Try playing these and seeing just how they sound to you.

One basic analytical first step would be to **just find the common tones** between the G Mixolydian mode and the D altered dominant scale. At a glance, those tones would be D, F, and C. Then, try examining the blue notes, and B♭/A♯ becomes an option. Now, try to improvise an idea that focuses on one of those pitches. Attempt to use that pitch/note as a pivot into the D7 altered dominant area even though G is still your harmonic center—your pedal tone. See how this sounds to you! Next, try to create a small motif using just the notes D, F, and C; perhaps doing this will actually make it easier to travel to other areas of implied harmony. In the recorded example, **Track 23,** you can hear that this was what I tried to do within a very brief amount of time.

Next, you could extend this process until you've explored all the possibilities. This could take quite some time. Just be patient with all the aspects, and simply take your time! I also suggest the **usage of small motifs** derived from playing chromatic upper and lower neighbors to the modal or blues-based tones and hear where they could take you.

Another option for experimentation over an extended vamp is to imagine that the G7 chord **could** be going to a C major or C minor chord. It could even be a ♭5 substitute for a D♭7 and be headed for a G♭maj7 or G♭m7. The key to this is that it's all really functioning as a false cadence because it will never actually resolve, but for the sake of analysis everything to the right of home base is the alteration of G altered dominant 7th, which gives you many more potential altered and outside options. I really hope this will help you get started, so it becomes a point of departure. Again, my improvised example was intended to be a composite of some of the suggested techniques.

What I have been presenting thus far in this unit is really the simple insertion of one chord change where it doesn't exist in the written music. However, with your imagination, you can take this idea several steps further and put into use a series of chord changes that could either take you from harmonic Point A to Point B or from Point A back to Point A. For instance, here in our example we are just vamping on a G pedal, which we are saying is a G7 chord. But, instead of just thinking of going to an outer area of D7(alt), what if you inserted a ♭5 substitute ii–V with your lines and alluded to E♭m7–A♭7? What if you went a step further and placed, in front of that chord change, another ii–V, Fm7–B♭7? You would then have Fm7–B♭7–E♭m7–A♭7, all two beats each before landing back at G7. Or you might want to go the other way around by playing lines that suggested B♭m–E♭7–E♭m7–A♭7; again, each chord change would probably be played for two beats before resolving to G7. You could also take this very same idea and use only altered dominant 7th chords, making it a V-of-V situation. This would look like E♭7(alt.)–A♭7(alt.) and back to G7, or it could be extended to F7(alt.)–B♭7(alt.)–E♭7(alt.)–A♭7(alt.) and back to G7. The key thing to remember is that you are playing lines that **suggest** these chord changes—but only because you hear them with your imagination, and the will of your line directs you in such a way. Try these very ideas using your pentatonics and see what it sounds like. Never forget that in this area of making music, anything is possible because your **imagination is king!**

USING THE CD: To hear my example improvisation, play **Track 23.** First, you will hear that I sought to establish that we were in the area of **G7.** What I then attempted to do as the improvisation developed was to go to several of these outer areas, suggested in the prior text, using the notes C, D, and F as my windows to move to and from the tonal center of G. When you feel ready to experiment with this particular approach to improvising, use **Track 24.** But you could also go to the **BLUE CD** from **CONTEMPORARY CHORD KHANCEPTS** and play along with **Tracks 16, 20,** and **26.** This will give you two different feels and tempos.

Example 15: Around and Outside the Consonant

im7 (Cm7)

G altered dominant/
A♭ melodic minor
(G, A♭, B♭, B/C♭, D♭, E♭, F)
C harmonic minor
(C, D, E♭, F, G, A♭, B)

Imaj7 (Cmaj7)

G altered dominant/
A♭ melodic minor
(G, A♭, B♭, B/C♭, D♭, E♭, F)

B♭ minor pentatonic
(B♭, D♭, E♭, F, A♭)
F minor pentatonic
(F, A♭, B♭, C, E♭)
D♭ dominant 7th pentatonic
(D♭, E♭, F, A♭, C♭)
E♭ dominant 7th pentatonic
(E♭, F, G, B♭, D♭)

Other options:

G half-tone/whole-tone
diminished scale
(G, A♭, B♭, B, C♯, D, E, F)
G whole-tone
(G, A, B, C♯, D♯, F)

V7 (alt.)

D7 (alt.)

D altered dominant/
E♭ melodic minor
(D, E♭, F, F♯/G♭, A♭, B♭, C)

Other options:

D half-tone/whole-tone
diminished scale
(D, E♭, F, F♯, A♭, A, B, C)
D whole-tone
(D, E, F♯, G♯, A♯, C)

F minor pentatonic
(F, A♭, B♭, C, E♭)
C minor pentatonic
(C, E♭, F, G, B♭)
A♭ dominant 7th pentatonic
(A♭, B♭, C, E♭, G♭)
B♭ dominant 7th pentatonic
(B♭, C, D, F, A♭)

Full Modes:

F Dorian/G Phrygian
(F, G, A♭, B♭, C, D, E♭)
C Dorian (plagal cadence)
(C, D, E♭, F, G, A, B♭)

I7	V7 (alt.)

G7

(G Mixolydian)
(G, A, B, C, D, E, F)

Blue Notes   [B♭]   [D♭]

G Lydian ♭7 Scale/
D melodic minor
(G, A, B, C♯, D, E, F)

A dominant 7th pentatonic
(A, B, C♯, E, G)

Though I was not blessed with particularly large hands or spindly fingers, I felt that it was essential that I offer an alternative to the basic pentatonic fingerings that align themselves to the more elementary concept of **one-finger-per-fret.** During the early '70s, just after I had moved to New York and began to take students, a young guitarist walked-in and showed me some pentatonic fingerings that seemed to be of his own invention, because he had a huge set of hands and could play across any one string with ease. Since that time, I have periodically made the effort to learn to play like this, but there are finger-ings presented here that I simply cannot play in the lower positions because the stretches between the fingers are simply too great. So, for those of you with small hands, don't be discouraged. Try to play what you can play comfortably; and with those fingerings that seem to have too great a gap, try to alter one of those tones to another correct modal note. The following is an example of how I've tried to solve this kind of problem.

Notice in our example of G7, looking at the dominant 7th pentatonic fingerings, at least once in each of the five fingerings a line begins with the third: B. This means that across that string as B goes to D and then goes to F, each one of those intervals is a minor 3rd and will have two frets between each note. It's a huge stretch from your first finger to your pinky to cover all of it. For me to make use of this in a real playing situation, I would change each B to a C so, for that moment, I am using a fingering for one string derived from the minor 7th pentatonic fingering. In the end, you would want to do something like this to keep your lines from sounding too homogeneous.

Here's an explanation of my harmonic thinking as it relates to this presentation. I've chosen the dominant 7th chord as the starting point. As I have stated throughout this text, I have adopted a minor orientation (using the Dorian mode and the melodic minor scales) to just about everything I do as it applies to improvising. Where a dominant 7th chord is con-cerned, if you were to start building up the harmony in thirds from the 5th degree, you would automatically be adding virtually all the consonant color tones: 7th, 9th, 11th, and 13th. So, in our example of G7, if I leave the bass note, the root (R), to the bassist and play either Dm7(9) chords or lines with a Dm7 (Dorian) orientation, I would already be extending the sound of the existing harmony.

This is why each section begins with the dominant 7th pentatonic lines and is then followed by the m7 lines derived from the ii chord of the major key or built from the 5th degree of the Mixolydian mode. Again, if our example is a G7 chord, we are in the key of C major, and the ii chord would be Dm7. G7 would produce the G Mixolydian mode, and Dm7 would pro-duce the D Dorian mode. And, since they are in the same key, they still have the same seven notes, just different starting points so that the crucial half steps fall in different places.

In this application, by using the D minor pentatonic over the G7, the only note you're adding to the G dominant 7th pentatonic is C (the 4th or 11th). It replaces the B, the 3rd of the chord, and serves to create a more open sense of harmony. In the final grouping present-ed, what I've offered is not a pentatonic scale; at times, it's really like playing the Lydian ♭7 scale across the strings, which in my orientation is like playing the melodic minor. In this case, that would be D melodic minor (D, E, F, G, A, B, C♯). In other words, the G Lydian ♭7 scale is the same as D melodic minor. Now, the C, which was introduced with the minor pentatonic, becomes C♯ (the ♭5) and further serves to extend the harmony. As you become more and more comfortable with the technical aspects of this concept born of an exercise, try then to put it to use in the context of the music you have been playing. See if it can truly work for you. This concept becomes a way of taking the ordinary aspects of the pentaton-ics and turning them into something extraordinary while again teaching your ears to hear things through your hands. Just give it a try and see how it sounds to you.

Unit Fourteen

Example 16: Pentatonic Stretch Fingerings
(Three across a string)

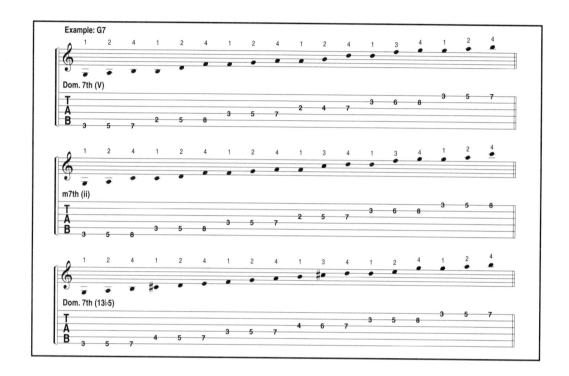

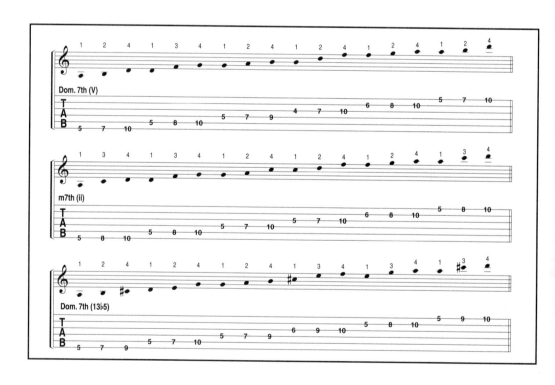

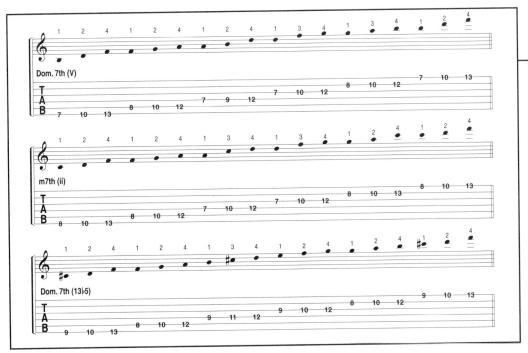

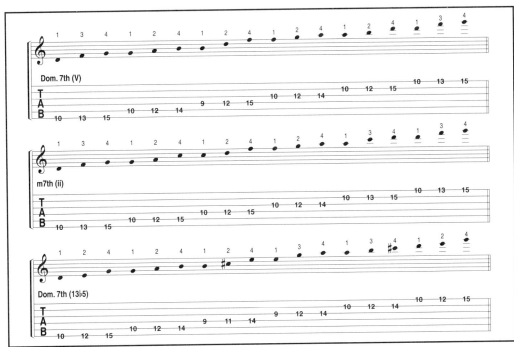

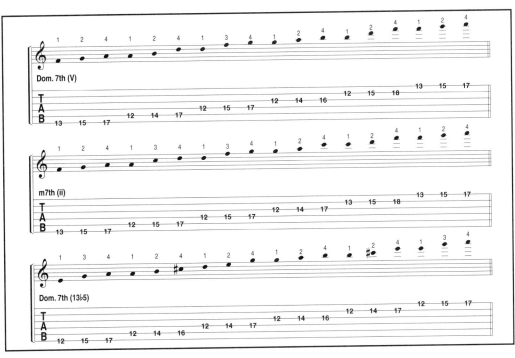

Pentatonic Khancepts

USING THE CD: These examples were not performed, so when you feel like practicing to something rhythmic and with a tonal center, use **Track 24.** However, you can also use **Tracks 20** and **26** from the **BLUE CD** that comes with the prior book, **CONTEMPORARY CHORD KHANCEPTS.** All of these tracks use G as the tonal center, which is as it should be because the examples were all written with G7 as the basic harmonic area.

Example 16: Pentatonic Stretch Fingering Exercises

Ex. 16A

Ex. 16B

Steve Khan

As stated before, playing in a one-dimensional pentatonic style of improvising is not going to make you sound like a "jazz" player. Remember that the language of jazz is unique. In order to speak that language fluently, you must master the nuances. However, because most of us begin to improvise from a scale-oriented (or mode-oriented) concept, the lines we play tend to be all too similar in character. The notes tend to be grouped together closely, absent of wide intervallic leaps. By adding pentatonic concepts to our playing, we are adding more intervallic space between the notes. This, in part, is because we are now employing five notes instead of seven!

This is where we can now take advantage of some of the special qualities in the way the notes of the pentatonics lay out on the fingerboard of the guitar. I've designed a series of example exercises using a string-skipping discipline to highlight larger interval jumps and also to serve as a challenge to your dexterity. For the purposes of employing these concepts, I've given examples as they might be used over both the iim7–V7(alt.)–Imaj progression [Cm7–F7(alt.)–B♭maj7] and the iim7(♭5)–V7(alt.)–im7 progression [Am7(♭5)–D7(alt.)–Gm7].

For the most part, these examples all use a stream of consecutive running eighth-notes, but this is not how you would normally improvise using this concept. What I am really hoping is that, by using these pentatonics, you will be able to develop your own relationship with each note you play over any chord family. That 'romance' you create with these notes then affects **what** you choose to play, and **when** you choose to play it. It should never be related to any exercise you might have learned, such as this one! With the examples presented, we are usually alternating between the D-string and B-string and the G-string and E-string. You would certainly want to extend this concept to include sounds created between the low E-string and the D-string as well as the A-string and the G-string. I chose to keep the sounds on the higher strings so that the notes would speak well when played against the play-along CD.

The other technical aspect I've tried to adhere to as a discipline is to keep the successive pentatonics as close together on the fingerboard as is possible, so that the sounds align themselves with the 'look' of how they are played. Again, in concept, your guitar fingerboard should resemble the way a keyboard might look to a pianist. It would make your fingerboard seem, at times, to be very compact, making your movements concise. It should feel as though the notes are right underneath your fingers at all times, and that radical, or dramatic movements are not required. Perhaps, over time, such movements would be found to be mostly unnecessary.

USING THE CD: Examples 17A–D appear on **Track 15** *after* the second four-bar space that I left just after **Examples 13A–D** were performed (2:16 into the track). Again, you will hear that each four-bar example was performed twice before I moved on to the next one. When you feel ready to try playing the examples yourself or just want to improvise using these new concepts, play along with **Track 16.**

Example 17: String–Skipping Exercises (ii–V–I) CD Track 15 CD Track 16

Ex. 17A

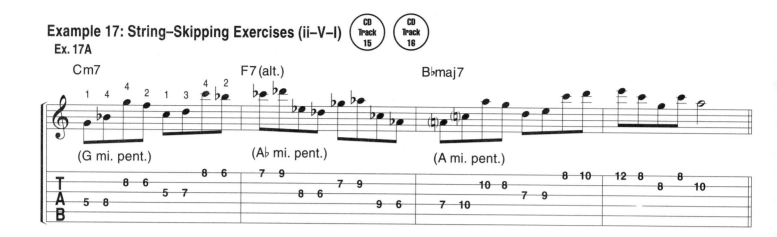

Ex. 17B

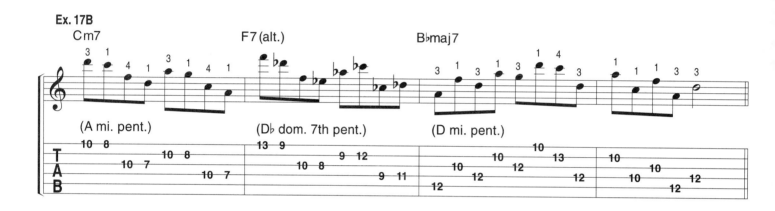

Ex. 17C

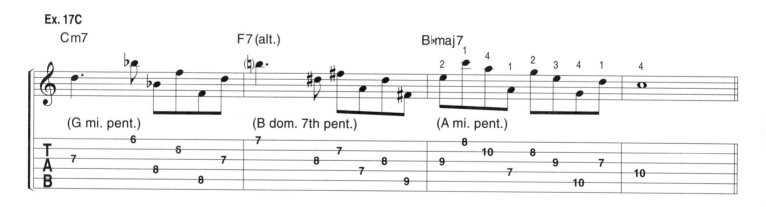

Ex. 17D

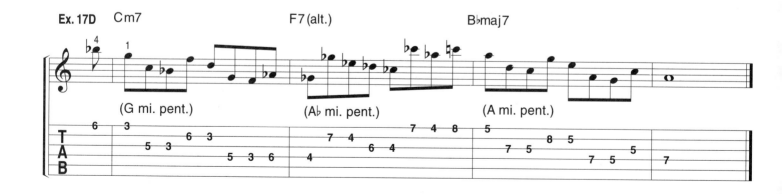

USING THE CD: Examples **18A–D** appear on **Track 17** after the four-bar vamp that follows Examples **14A–D** (2:25 into the track). When you feel ready to try playing the examples yourself or just want to improvise using these new concepts, play along with **Track 18.**

Example 18: String-Skipping Exercises (iim7(♭5)–V–i)

Ex. 18A

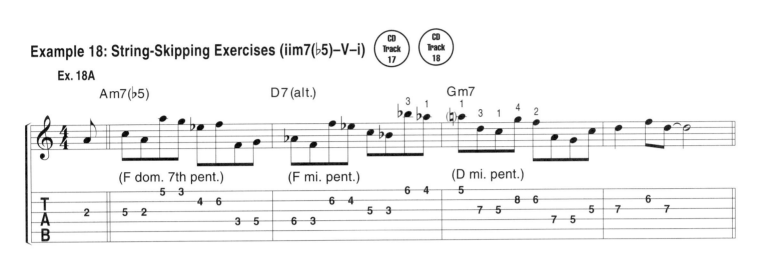

Ex. 18B

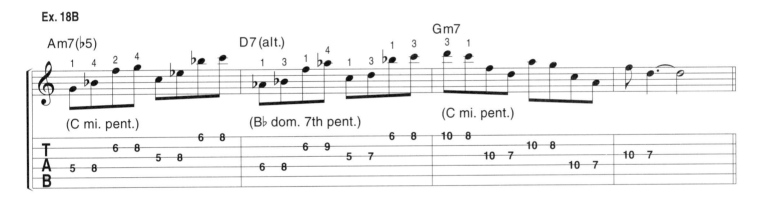

Ex. 18C

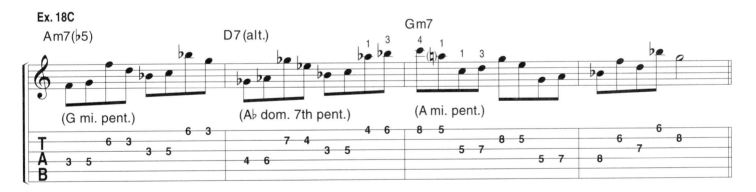

Ex. 18D

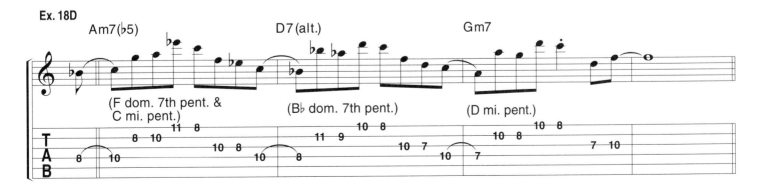

UNIT SIXTEEN
The Doubled-Note Effect

What could be considered a by-product of the pentatonic stretch fingerings we examined in **Unit 15** is what I call the doubled-note effect. I believe that, as guitarists, this is our method of approximating sounds that might be most associated with saxophonists and trumpet players. During the course of an improvisation, this effect gets put to use when a player is riding one note over several bars with accents and allowing the rhythm section to really intensify the feeling underneath. When this effect is notated, we usually use the plus sign (+) above the alternating notes; one of them would be heard as sounding just slightly different. On woodwind (saxophones and flutes) and brass (trumpet and trombone) instruments, as with the guitar, the effect is accomplished by playing the same note with an alternate fingering.

For guitarists, this effect is most easily accomplished by playing the same note on both your B string and G string. For example, play the note D on your B string with your first finger on the 3rd fret, and then reach out with your pinky or third finger and play the note D on your G string. Once this is under your fingers comfortably, try alternating these notes while building up velocity. With this safely understood, then try adding the blue note of D♭/C♯, which would appear on the 6th fret of your G string (one fret below the D you had been playing). This should add some bluesiness to what you had just played.

By using the stretch fingerings across several sets of strings, your opportunities for putting this effect into use are increased. If you look at most of the fingerings offered, you can clearly see that the note upon which you end on any consecutive string becomes the first note on the next string, both ascending and descending. As you learn to play these kinds of fingerings with greater speed, the effect of the doubled note becomes increasingly subtle. Please give it a try!

Example 19: Doubled-Note Effect

D Minor Pentatonic

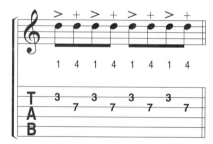 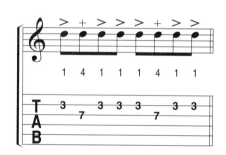

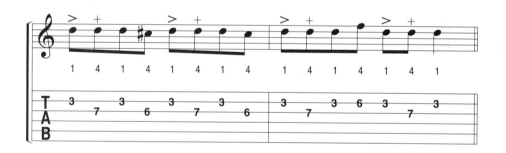

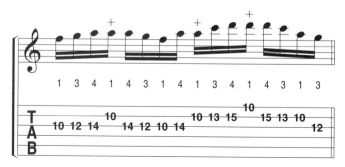 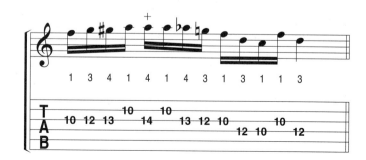

Steve Khan

Every generation of players has some preoccupation with virtuosity, the development of greater facility—the ability to execute musical ideas with speed, complete fluidity, and confidence. Therefore, the following examples are suggestions for some very basic velocity exercises to aid in the development of your speed and facility. Executing runs and flurries of notes with good time and speed can be very impressive—but never lose sight of how much more effective they are if you can end with a beautiful sounding note.

To conserve space because of the tab format, many of the exercise suggestions are offered in partial form, leaving them to be completed by you. Also, they are offered only in one of the five positions. So, this is where the sincerity and will of your efforts is going to come into play. It will not serve you well to be a "master" in only one position. You must make the effort to take the basic concept from one position and then apply it to the other four. If you make that effort, you will, without question, be far the better for it.

It is also crucial to make the effort not only to learn and master all things related to the usage and employment of the minor pentatonic but also to apply the same efforts to the dominant 7th pentatonic. In addition to these essentials, the blues scale should be examined and applied so that it might be connected to both of our main pentatonics. While this book strives to provide you with an angular option to your improvised lines, it is also my goal to bring you closer to the earthiness and soulfulness of the blues language. Please don't lose sight of this.

[1] Groupings of Six Notes (Ascending and Descending)

You may already be very familiar with fingering the minor pentatonics because of our experiences in rock, heavy metal, and jazz-rock fusion, but if this material is new to you, I've tried to present some very simple and fundamental velocity exercises (intended to develop speed and facility) with both the minor and dominant 7th pentatonics. The examples are presented using only the first position (the position lowest on the neck), so if you become inspired to do so, expand each one to the other four positions as they were presented in **Unit 1.**

Example 20: G Minor Pentatonic

Ex. 20A

Ex. 20B

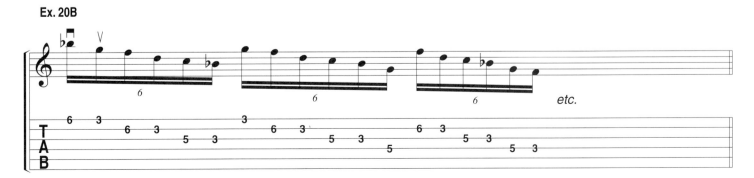

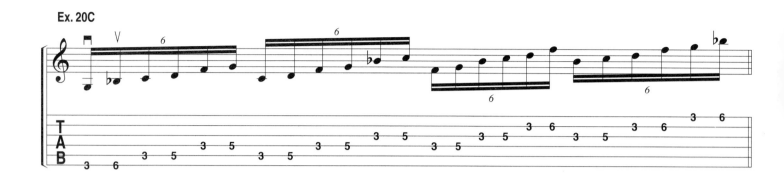

Ex. 20C

Ex. 20D

Example 21: C Dominant 7th Pentatonic

Ex. 21A

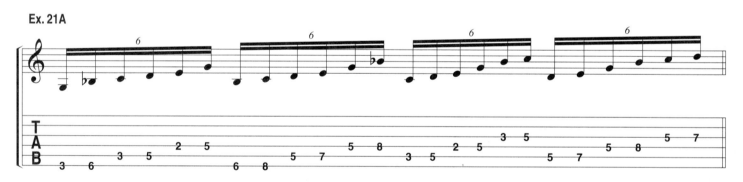

Ex. 21B

Steve Khan

Ex. 21C

Ex. 21D

Example 22: Classic Line/Pattern

Ex. 22A

(G mi. pent.)

Ex. 22B

(C dom. 7th pent.)

[2] Ascending and Descending on Two Strings

The following exercises are presented so that you will never lose sight of the horizontal aspects of the guitar (playing up and down the neck). Most of the materials presented in this book put to use the vertical approach, playing across the strings, since it offers the most economy of motion. In the course of real improvising, however, your lines are going to take you on some unexpected journeys and you must be prepared for that as well. It's the principle of the music playing you as opposed to you playing the music.

These examples are presented using only the G string and B string for simplicity's sake, but as we ascend or descend the fingerboard, we pass through all five pentatonic fingerings for both the minor and dominant 7th forms. These all could be played by using alternate picking techniques for a more machine-gun type of attack or by only lightly striking the first note on each string and playing the second note as a hammer-on, which would give a decidedly more legato feeling to your lines.

Example 23: Ascending Two-String Exercise

Ex. 23A

(G mi. pent.)

Ex. 23B

(C dom. 7th pent.)

Descending:

Ex. 23C

(G mi. pent.)

Ex. 23D

(C dom. 7th pent.)

[3] Sixteenth Notes Across Six Strings

If you just can't get enough of disciplined practicing, this exercise will be perfect for you. It moves sequentially through the five notes of the pentatonic and forces you to negotiate that sequence across all six guitar strings. You can probably gain the most from this by shifting the accents from the downbeats of each quarter note to any of the sixteenth notes that follow.

Example 24: Minor Pentatonic Velocity in Sixteenth Notes

Ex. 24A

(G mi. pent.)

Dominant 7th Velocity in Sixteenth Notes

Ex. 24B

(C dom. 7th pent.)

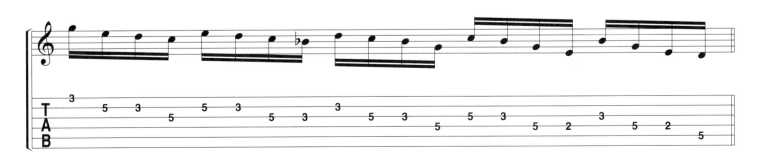

[4] Dominant 7th

This is a special series of exercises that, for the purpose of presenting as much material as possible in this book, span only the top two three-string groupings of the guitar. If you want to pursue this further, you could expand the exercise to include playing across your A through G strings and, finally, your low E through D strings.

One interesting idea to explore is using one of the pitches as a pivot tone and then rotating the pentatonics around that pitch. For example, if you were to look at the first C7 position presented, you would go down from B♭-G-E-C and then B♭ again. But if you went from B♭-A♭-F♭-D♭-C♭, would have outlined the upper extensions of a G♭9 chord. If you then tried to go from B♭-A♭-F-D-C and back, you would have outlined a B♭9. Again, give this idea a try and see what you come up with.

However, the real issue here is that a dominant 7th chord is almost always coming from somewhere—a iim7 or II7 chord—and is headed somewhere as well—a Imaj7 or im7. If you re-examine how the dominant 7th pentatonic is used over altered dominant 7th chords, you would recall that it could either be the ♭5 or ♯5 of that root. So, as we're using C dominant 7th pentatonic as our example, it would be ♭5 of G♭/F♯7(alt.), which means it is headed toward a Bmaj7 or Bm7. It would also be the ♯5 of E7(alt.), which means it is headed to Amaj7 or Am7. So, when practicing these velocity studies, just imagine that you are headed to one of those areas and make the proper resolutions. Remember, if the possibilities do not immediately come to mind, make the effort and write out your own charts. That's the best way to learn.

Example 25: Dominant 7th Pentatonic Velocity Study

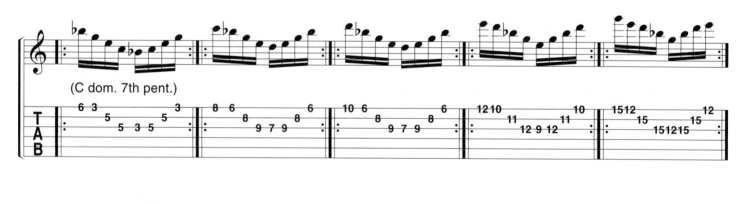

(C dom. 7th pent.)

[5] Combinations: Minor Pentatonic and Dominant 7th Pentatonic

As I mentioned in the Introduction, I used to spend hours listening to McCoy Tyner's solos when he was part of John Coltrane's great quartet from the mid-'60s. I was fascinated by how he would intermingle the two pentatonics within his lines. The following examples are just suggestions for how you might begin to explore the usage of both the minor and dominant 7th pentatonics in combination so that they don't always function as separate entities within your lines. You can certainly hear these devices and configurations in the guitar lines of John McLaughlin when he performed and recorded with his Mahavishnu Orchestra and later with Shakti.

USING THE CD: Since all the presented velocity examples use either G minor pentatonic and/or C dominant 7th pentatonic, you should play them over a C pedal or a G pedal to get the fullest sense of how they sound in context. So, use **Tracks 2** or **24.**

Example 26: Combinations: Minor and Dominant 7th Pentatonics

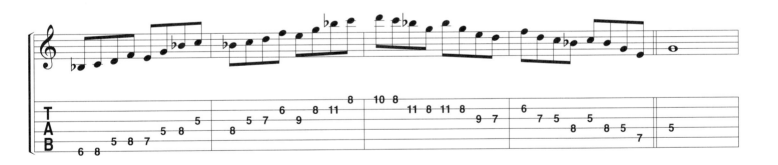

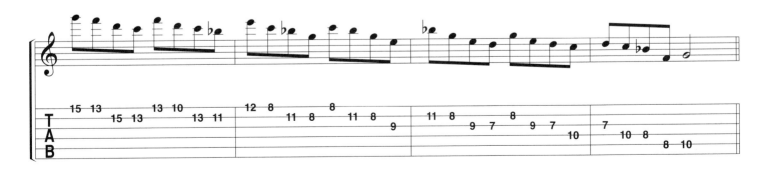

UNIT EIGHTEEN
Improvising Over "Standard" Changes ─────────────────────

When you are presented with a new piece of music and you are told that some-where within the composition you will have to take a solo, first try to get a brief overview of the composition as a whole. Look at the simple things:

1] **How long is it? How many pages?**

2] **Is it in any kind of a key (w/a key signature), and does that matter?**

3] **How many sections does it contain?**

4] **Where does your solo appear?**

5] **Are there any melodies you must play?**

Once you have answered these basic questions to your satisfaction, take a longer look at your solo section. Depending upon just how many chords you will have to negotiate, you may even want to do a more detailed analysis by writing down some helpful hints on your part. If there are a lot of chords, this can really speed up the process of being able to **hear through the changes** sooner. First take a look at each individual chord and assign it a mode or scale name based upon the letter name and chord color (the chord family of the root). If you want to take that even further, convert some of them to either the Dorian mode or the melodic minor scale since you have altered your orientation so that just about every-thing is thought of in minor. This has proved to be simple and successful for me. With those steps taken, go a step further and add in all of the minor and dominant 7th pentatonic pos-sibilities. Once that's done, look through the relationships of the chords to one another and try to prepare yourself to hear through them by looking for common tones and common pentatonic relationships, which can really help and can keep your improvisations close to a blues-based sound and feeling. With these suggestions now in hand, we will soon take a closer analytical look at the four improvised tunes shown in **Examples 27, 30, 31,** and **32** and view their linear and pentatonic possibilities.

In previous chapters, we took an in-depth look at the most important chord families and the possibilities for pentatonic improvising. This included looking at the altered dominant 7th chord and how it resolves to any number of chordal destinations. Finally, we examined cadences to both major and minor. In a sense, you should be prepared to attack most musi-cal situations with these new improvisational tools. While preparing the materials for this book, my publisher and I thought it was important to create a work that is inclusive and does not shut out any player or any genre. Though I am known as a jazz musician and jazz guitarist, I didn't want that designation to make musicians from the worlds of rock, pop, blues, R&B, hip-hop, and country music feel that there is nothing useful here for them. The difficult thing with any publication is space—just how much information can fit in any one book. I used five pieces of music, including two blues progressions, so as not to exclude anyone and yet offer the harmonic complexities to challenge jazz players of all levels as well. I hope I succeeded in accomplishing this goal.

The musical examples and the corresponding tracks from the play-along CD are intended to provide you with the skills to make any improvising situation considerably easier. What you're going to see in all the examples is what I would do **if** I were having problems under-standing just how to approach a progression over which I might have to solo. For clarity I have gone into greater detail than I would have for just myself. I hope that your being able to view this process will enable you to do the same thing or something similar to help your-self.

When I am first handed any new piece of music or told that we might be playing a standard of some sort, if it's something I'm totally unfamiliar with, I often neatly write out everything again for myself. In a sense, what I'm doing is creating a worksheet very much like what I've done for you, at least in part, in each of the following examples. Underneath each of the chord changes, I write out all my improvising possibilities. First, I always begin by making certain that the correct mode or scale corresponds with the chord symbol. What you should remember from this book and from **CONTEMPORARY CHORD KHANCEPTS** is that, gen-erally speaking, I convert everything, with few exceptions, to minor. I then use either the

Dorian mode or the melodic minor scale. However, I always first label the mode in terms of how it applies to the root name of the chord. It is always important to first understand these relationships before converting any of them to your own system of musical organization. Once that is done, I then list all of my pentatonic possibilities just below, usually trying to go in order of the ones that I feel might sound best.

The next and final step is to begin to see the piece of music as a whole. We want to understand the flow of the chord changes, how they move in and out of one another. In doing this part of my preparation, I first look to see just what the **common tones** are, if any, between the mode/scale I am in and the next one because the common tones will give continuity to the lines and keep them from sounding disconnected. From a rhythmic perspective, this will enable your lines to sound as if they were flowing **over the bar lines** and not being approached as if each individual chord change was operating within its own small harmonic box. While I was performing a solo for Steely Dan many years ago, Donald Fagen offered some criticism by saying: "Steve, the solo sounds kind of boxey to me." At that time, I had never heard this expression before, and in truth, I haven't heard it since. But I have come to understand exactly what he meant. He was asking me to **play over the bar lines** and **through the changes** rather than approaching them as if they were each in individual harmonic boxes. Though I was just getting familiar and comfortable with the tune and its changes, his direction was very helpful. Sometimes when preparing to solo over something I've never seen before, I will even go so far as to use as many as five colored highlighter marking pens to make these harmonic images even more visual by coloring in the common tones. Once I do this, I then look through all the various pentatonic options I've created, searching to answer a couple of fundamental questions: **[1]** are there any pentatonics that stay the same from one chord change to the next? And **[2]** are there any pentatonics that are only a half step, or even a whole step away from each other? When we were examining **Pentatonic Improvising Over Cadences** in **Units 11** and **12,** I would have made these exact same suggestions. So, in a sense, even if this is all new material to you, by now you should be a bit more familiar with some of these options.

Now, let's take a look at the musical examples.

DENZALÓN

This example, which employs the simple movement from **major to minor** and back again, is very important. What we are doing here in this portion of **PENTATONIC KHANCEPTS** should work hand-in-hand with all you might have gained from your work in **Unit 15** (page 48) of **CONTEMPORARY CHORD KHANCEPTS.** If you are still wondering about just how far-reaching this type of exercise can be for your ability to better hear your improvisations, revisit that chapter from the earlier book.

Since this is the first song example here, I have taken steps to prepare you for improvising over such chordal movements, movements that occur in countless "real" standards from the pop and jazz repertoire. Below each chord change, you will see your modal options and your pentatonic options presented clearly. The purpose is to alleviate the amount of initial thinking you might have to do and to enable you to begin to improvise freely without, perhaps, fully understanding exactly **why** your playing sounds so good—which is something you must attempt to explore and understand from this point forward.

USING THE CD: When you want to hear my improvisation over **Example 27,** play **Track 25.** When you are ready to try improvising over this sample progression, use **Track 26.**

Example 27: Denzalón

Mode/Scale Options:

A major/Lydian
(A, B, C♯, D/D♯, E, F♯, G♯)

Pentatonic Options:

C♯ minor pentatonic
(C♯, E, F♯, G♯, B)
G♯ minor pentatonic
(G♯, B, C♯, D♯, F♯)
F♯ minor pentatonic
(F♯, A, B, C♯, E)

Mode/Scale Options:

A Dorian
(A, B, C, D, E, F♯, G)

Pentatonic Options:

A minor pentatonic
(A, C, D, E, G)
B minor pentatonic
(B, D, E, F♯, A)
E minor pentatonic
(E, G, A, B, D)
D dominant 7th pentatonic
(D, E, F♯, A, C)

KHALATMO

This example offers a simple but terrific workout over dominant 7th chords. Though it's not a blues, it's close enough to provide a challenge for players of all styles because the changes fall in an interesting manner. Essentially, you only have to deal with the I7 and IV7 chords, and this is what keeps it related to the blues feeling.

If you view your I7 (F7) chord as the mode based upon the root, you would have F Mixolydian, and then as that chord moves to the IV7 (B♭7), you would simply change the modal reference to F Dorian. In doing so, you've simply changed **one note,** 'A' has become 'A♭.' Other than staying the same, what could be more simple?

One place to begin in improving your ability to hear the usage of pentatonics as they "extend" the harmony would be to simply apply the minor pentatonic (based upon the ii chord) for each dominant 7th chord. This simply translates into the following:

[1] for F7 (V-type) use Cm (ii-type) pentatonic, and

[2] for B♭7 (V-type) use Fm (ii-type) pentatonic.

When doing this, try to keep both pentatonics **in the same position** on the guitar. It will be the best thing in the long term, giving you the sense of hearing what is really right beneath your fingers without unnecessary movement. If you studied **CONTEMPORARY CHORD KHANCEPTS,** this will all sound familiar because we were applying iim7 voicings above the root of the V7 to create more lush and extended harmonies. With your lines, it can and should be absolutely the same thing.

In examining the pentatonic possibilities, I also see that each chordal area offers the use of both G minor and C minor pentatonic, so you would want to work the usage of these pentatonics into your improvising to see just what they sound like. I also see that, if you were to use D minor pentatonic over the F7 chord, you could then go down a whole step and use the C minor pentatonic over the Bb7 chord. It's a simple movement that would add an angular quality to your soloing and give you an easy physical movement to make as these things lay out on the fingerboard. In a sense, it's as if your fingers are yet again teaching your ears how to **hear through the changes.**

If you want or need to hear my performed example, go to CD #2, the **RED CD,** from **CHORD KHANCEPTS** and listen to **Track 13.**

USING THE CD: Though this is a track that was used in the prior book, the blank track appears here in an abbreviated format. To play along using the concepts suggested in **Example 28,** play **Track 27.**

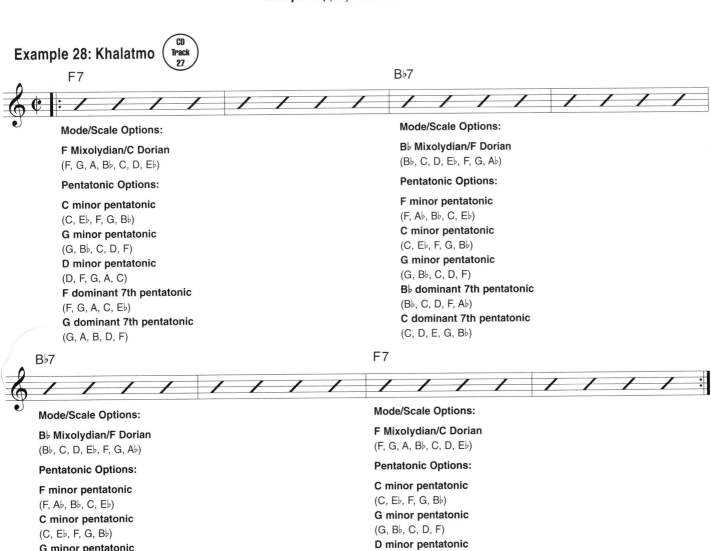

Example 28: Khalatmo (CD Track 27)

F7

Mode/Scale Options:

F Mixolydian/C Dorian
(F, G, A, Bb, C, D, Eb)

Pentatonic Options:

C minor pentatonic
(C, Eb, F, G, Bb)
G minor pentatonic
(G, Bb, C, D, F)
D minor pentatonic
(D, F, G, A, C)
F dominant 7th pentatonic
(F, G, A, C, Eb)
G dominant 7th pentatonic
(G, A, B, D, F)

Bb7

Mode/Scale Options:

Bb Mixolydian/F Dorian
(Bb, C, D, Eb, F, G, Ab)

Pentatonic Options:

F minor pentatonic
(F, Ab, Bb, C, Eb)
C minor pentatonic
(C, Eb, F, G, Bb)
G minor pentatonic
(G, Bb, C, D, F)
Bb dominant 7th pentatonic
(Bb, C, D, F, Ab)
C dominant 7th pentatonic
(C, D, E, G, Bb)

Bb7

Mode/Scale Options:

Bb Mixolydian/F Dorian
(Bb, C, D, Eb, F, G, Ab)

Pentatonic Options:

F minor pentatonic
(F, Ab, Bb, C, Eb)
C minor pentatonic
(C, Eb, F, G, Bb)
G minor pentatonic
(G, Bb, C, D, F)
Bb dominant 7th pentatonic
(Bb, C, D, F, Ab)
C dominant 7th pentatonic
(C, D, E, G, Bb)

F7

Mode/Scale Options:

F Mixolydian/C Dorian
(F, G, A, Bb, C, D, Eb)

Pentatonic Options:

C minor pentatonic
(C, Eb, F, G, Bb)
G minor pentatonic
(G, Bb, C, D, F)
D minor pentatonic
(D, F, G, A, C)
F dominant 7th pentatonic
(F, G, A, C, Eb)
G dominant 7th pentatonic
(G, A, B, D, F)

A SHADE OF TJADE (Blues in G)

This is the first of two example blues progressions, and it is intended to be the more simple of the two. Essentially, you're dealing with only three dominant 7th chordal areas, offering you plenty of time to explore each chord change. Much of what I mentioned in the prior example, "Khalatmo," holds true here as well, since the relationship from G7 to C7 is the same as it is from F7 to Bb7. You are just moving the ideas up a whole step.

To begin expanding your ability to hear the usage of these pentatonics, which will extend your sense of harmony, simply apply the minor pentatonic of the ii chord for each dominant 7th chord. This simply translates into the following:

[1] For G7(V-type), use Dm(ii-type) pentatonic.

[2] For C7(V-type), use Gm(ii-type) pentatonic.

[3] For D7(V-type), use Am(ii-type) pentatonic.

When doing this, try to keep all three pentatonics **in the same position** on the guitar. It will be the best thing in the long term, giving the sense of hearing what is really right beneath your fingers without unnecessary movement.

Though you do not have to observe the following theories to sound good, here are some additional ideas you can explore. Since **bar 4** is one of the most crucial bars in any blues progression, it offers great possibilities, for it is the bar where your I7 chord truly becomes a dominant 7th chord as it pushes towards a resolution to the IV7 chord. So, to increase the tension in your lines, try either of the two following ideas: **[1]** simply use the G altered dominant scale (Ab melodic minor to some) to create the harmonic tension that would then be released upon resolution, and **[2]** just play the Dorian mode (Ab Dorian) one half step above where you are (G7) or the Mixolydian mode (Db Mixolydian) a half step above where you are headed (C7). By doing this, you create a circumstance whereby your lines can resolve easily, almost effortlessly, one half step downward. This is a device often associated with the great saxophonist John Coltrane. In the tune that follows this example though it's a blues in Bb, this very idea is actually written into the changes at **bar 4.** Here, however, as in most cases, it is not. And it actually makes the shape and thrust of your lines even more important because the need for resolution is greater.

If you're making a careful study of all of these options, you will notice that if you use the Ab melodic minor, it will have all the "correct" notes. But if you're employing Ab Dorian, the difference of having the Gb occur is huge—it would be considered a "wrong" note by most people because it is actually the major 7th (F♯), which does not exist in any form of a G7 chord! However, if it's tucked within your line, it can pass by almost unnoticed. So, be careful with it and where it falls rhythmically.

USING THE CD: This track was also used in the prior book; the blank track appears here, again in a more abbreviated format. To play along, using the concepts suggested in **Example 29,** use **Track 28.**

Example 29: A Shade of Tjade

Opt.

G7

[G7(alt.)]

Mode/Scale Options:

G Mixolydian/D Dorian
(G, A, B, C, D, E, F)

Pentatonic Options:

D minor pentatonic
(D, F, G, A, C)
A minor pentatonic
(A, C, D, E, G)
E minor pentatonic
(E, G, A, B, D)
G dominant 7th pentatonic
(G, A, B, D, F)
A dominant 7th pentatonic
(A, B, C♯, E, G)

Mode/Scale Options:

G altered dominant/
A♭ melodic minor
(G, A♭, B♭, B/C♭, D♭, E♭, F)

Pentatonic Options:

B♭ minor pentatonic
(B♭, D♭, E♭, F, A♭)
D♭ dominant 7th pentatonic
(D♭, E♭, F, A♭, C♭)
E♭ dominant 7th pentatonic
(E♭, F, G, B♭, D♭)

Mode/Scale Options:

A♭ Dorian/D♭ Mixolydian
(A♭, B♭, C♭, D♭, E♭, F, [G♭])

Pentatonic Options:

A♭ minor pentatonic
(A♭, C♭, D♭, E♭, [G♭])
E♭ minor pentatonic
(E♭, [G♭], A♭, B♭, D♭)
B♭ minor pentatonic
(B♭, D♭, E♭, F, A♭)
D♭ dominant 7th pentatonic
(D♭, E♭, F, A♭, C♭)

C7

G7

Mode/Scale Options:

C Mixolydian/G Dorian
(C, D, E, F, G, A, B♭)

Pentatonic Options:

G minor pentatonic
(G, B♭, C, D, F)
D minor pentatonic
(D, F, G, A, C)
A minor pentatonic
(A, C, D, E, G)
C dominant 7th pentatonic
(C, D, E, G, B♭)
D dominant 7th pentatonic
(D, E, F♯, A, C)

Mode/Scale Options:

G Mixolydian/D Dorian
(G, A, B, C, D, E, F)

Pentatonic Options:

D minor pentatonic
(D, F, G, A, C)
A minor pentatonic
(A, C, D, E, G)
E minor pentatonic
(E, G, A, B, D)
G dominant 7th pentatonic
(G, A, B, D, F)
A dominant 7th pentatonic
(A, B, C♯, E, G)

D7

C7

G7

Mode/Scale Options:

D Mixolydian/A Dorian
(D, E, F♯, G, A, B, C)

Pentatonic Options:

A minor pentatonic
(A, C, D, E, G)
E minor pentatonic
(E, G, A, B, D)
B minor pentatonic
(B, D, E, F♯, A)
D dominant 7th pentatonic
(D, E, F♯, A, C)
E dominant 7th pentatonic
(E, F♯, G♯, B, D)

Mode/Scale Options:

C Mixolydian/G Dorian
(C, D, E, F, G, A, B♭)

Pentatonic Options:

G minor pentatonic
(G, B♭, C, D, F)
D minor pentatonic
(D, F, G, A, C)
A minor pentatonic
(A, C, D, E, G)
C dominant 7th pentatonic
(C, D, E, G, B♭)
D dominant 7th pentatonic
(D, E, F♯, A, C)

Mode/Scale Options:

G Mixolydian/D Dorian
(G, A, B, C, D, E, F)

Pentatonic Options:

D minor pentatonic
(D, F, G, A, C)
A minor pentatonic
(A, C, D, E, G)
E minor pentatonic
(E, G, A, B, D)
G dominant 7th pentatonic
(G, A, B, D, F)
A dominant 7th pentatonic
(A, B, C♯, E, G)

MAD BUMPYVILLE (Blues in B♭)

This is the second of the two blues tracks to be presented here. And, in truth, as was mentioned during the discussion of the prior tune, the only real difference, other than that this piece is a blues in B♭, is that the **♭5 substitute iim7–V7 (Bm7–E7)** is actually written into the changes at **bar 4.** Remember that E7 is the ♭5 substitute for B♭7. So, in **bar 4,** you will now see that the bar has been divided with two beats each for Bm7 and E7. Since the bass is making these changes, you should hear a great difference, and everything I've suggested that you might choose to play will have greater harmonic clarity.

Another interesting spot for exploration in a blues such as this is **bar 8.** Depending upon how you view things, you could obviously stay right where you are, in this case on a B♭7 chord. However, you could also take the approach of thinking about where you are headed and then adjust your lines accordingly. By that I mean that in this blues we are headed for the V7 chord, F7. So, you could say to yourself, what is the V7 of the V chord? The answer here is a C7(alt.) chord of some sort. So, one idea you might try would be to insert lines that indicate that you are approaching this bar as a V7 of V7, even though no one else is looking at it in this fashion at that moment. Or, you might try this: We're approaching the F7 (V7) chord from the mode of the iim7 chord in that key area, that is to say, C Dorian, or Cm7. Now, you'd ask, what is the V7 chord of Cm7? It's G7(alt.). So, you also might try lines that allude to the V7 of the iim7. On play-along **Track 30,** during the first three choruses of this blues, you can best experiment with this device. Because the texture here is so open, with no string pads for chordal support, it creates a lot of space for this kind of experimentation. See what happens. If you're having problems understanding what your options might be, use the options I offer for C7(alt.) or G7(alt.) on other sample tunes, and go so far as to actually write in those options. This is the perfect moment to put that work method to use! The other key thing to remember is that employing ideas like this requires the use of your harmonic imagination, you have to begin to learn to hear lines, lines that indicate certain harmonic areas even if they don't exist as part of the chord changes, or the chord change in this case.

If you want or need to hear another performed example, go to **CD #2,** the **RED CD,** and listen to **Track 11.** Though for **CHORD KHANCEPTS,** the tune was titled "Sliceville," it is essentially the same piece of music. You will notice that I did not have the bass playing the substitute changes at **bar 4.** However, you can hear that I alluded to it, the Bm7–E7 change, with my lines. Over the course of this long improvisation, you are also able to hear how I like to employ line configurations that are sometimes outside of the expected consonant harmony, but they are always headed towards a resolution at some point. These are principles that were addressed thoroughly in **Unit 13.**

USING THE CD: To hear my improvisation over this particular type of blues progression, play **Track 29.** When you feel ready to improvise using the concepts from **Example 30,** play **Track 30.**

Example 30: Mad Bumpyville

B♭7   Bm7   E7

Mode/Scale Options:

B♭ Mixolydian/F Dorian
(B♭, C, D, E♭, F, G, A♭)

Pentatonic Options:

F minor pentatonic
(F, A♭, B♭, C, E♭)
C minor pentatonic
(C, E♭, F, G, B♭)
G minor pentatonic
(G, B♭, C, D, F)
B♭ dominant 7th pentatonic
(B♭, C, D, F, A♭)
C dominant 7th pentatonic
(C, D, E, G, B♭)

Mode/Scale Options:

B Dorian
(B, C♯, D, E, F♯, G♯, A)

Pentatonic Options:

B minor pentatonic
(B, D, E, F♯, A)
F♯ minor pentatonic
(F♯, A, B, C♯, E)
C♯ minor pentatonic
(C♯, E, F♯, G♯, B)
E dominant 7th pentatonic
(E, F♯, G♯, B, D)

E♭7   B♭7

Mode/Scale Options:

E♭ Mixolydian/B♭ Dorian
(E♭, F, G, A♭, B♭, C, D♭)

Pentatonic Options:

B♭ minor pentatonic
(B♭, D♭, E♭, F, A♭)
F minor pentatonic
(F, A♭, B♭, C, E♭)
C minor pentatonic
(C, E♭, F, G, B♭)
E♭ dominant 7th pentatonic
(E♭, F, G, B♭, D♭)
F dominant 7th pentatonic
(F, G, A, C, E♭)

Mode/Scale Options:

B♭ Mixolydian/F Dorian
(B♭, C, D, E♭, F, G, A♭)

Pentatonic Options:

F minor pentatonic
(F, A♭, B♭, C, E♭)
C minor pentatonic
(C, E♭, F, G, B♭)
G minor pentatonic
(G, B♭, C, D, F)
B♭ dominant 7th pentatonic
(B♭, C, D, F, A♭)
C dominant 7th pentatonic
(C, D, E, G, B♭)

F7   B♭7

Mode/Scale Options:

F Mixolydian/C Dorian
(F, G, A, B♭, C, D, E♭)

Pentatonic Options:

C minor pentatonic
(C, E♭, F, G, B♭)
G minor pentatonic
(G, B♭, C, D, F)
D minor pentatonic
(D, F, G, A, C)
F dominant 7th pentatonic
(F, G, A, C, E♭)
C dominant 7th pentatonic
(C, D, E, G, B♭)

Mode/Scale Options:

B♭ Mixolydian/F Dorian
(B♭, C, D, E♭, F, G, A♭)

Pentatonic Options:

F minor pentatonic
(F, A♭, B♭, C, E♭)
C minor pentatonic
(C, E♭, F, G, B♭)
G minor pentatonic
(G, B♭, C, D, F)
B♭ dominant 7th pentatonic
(B♭, C, D, F, A♭)
C dominant 7th pentatonic
(C, D, E, G, B♭)

BIG KAYAK

Some of you will recognize this piece as the changes to a relatively well-known Brazilian standard. I've chosen it for the book because of its compact form, only 16 bars, and it offers the chance to explore three different areas of major 7 chords and also a full I–VI(alt.)–iim7–V7(alt.) turnaround progression. Within those last four bars, you could even say you are using your knowledge of a V7–im and a V7–Imaj, since E7(alt.) resolves to Am7, and of course D7(alt.) resolves to Gmaj7 at the top of the tune. Though this is a topic better covered in depth in another book, try to keep in mind that, as an improviser, you would have all of your linear options available when an altered dominant 7th chord resolves to major. But when an altered dominant 7th chord resolves to minor, you have fewer, but very clear, options. When improvising and focusing just on your pentatonic possibilities, you'll find that, for the most part, any questionable notes have been simply left out of these five-note structures. Should you have remaining questions, please refer back to **Unit 9,** which dealt with your options in great depth.

If you look carefully at the harmonic movement of the first four bars, you'll see that this same movement is repeated twice, each time going down by a whole step: from G major to F major and from F major to E♭ major. And if you're looking to really simplify the movement in total, it's almost as if the progression were moving downward in half steps: Gmaj7–G♭ Mixolydian–Fmaj7–E Mixolydian–E♭maj7–D Mixolydian. If you explore all of your modal and then pentatonic possibilities carefully, you will find many interesting relationships that exist, and exist only a whole step apart.

USING THE CD: To listen to my performed improvisation over these changes, play **Track 31.** When you feel ready to create your own solos, use **Track 32.**

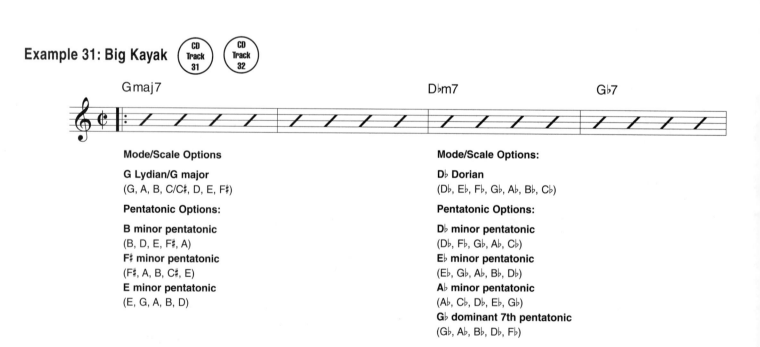

Example 31: Big Kayak

| Gmaj7 | | Dbm7 | Gb7 |

Mode/Scale Options

G Lydian/G major
(G, A, B, C/C♯, D, E, F♯)

Pentatonic Options:

B minor pentatonic
(B, D, E, F♯, A)
F♯ minor pentatonic
(F♯, A, B, C♯, E)
E minor pentatonic
(E, G, A, B, D)

Mode/Scale Options:

D♭ Dorian
(D♭, E♭, F♭, G♭, A♭, B♭, C♭)

Pentatonic Options:

D♭ minor pentatonic
(D♭, F♭, G♭, A♭, C♭)
E♭ minor pentatonic
(E♭, G♭, A♭, B♭, D♭)
A♭ minor pentatonic
(A♭, C♭, D♭, E♭, G♭)
G♭ dominant 7th pentatonic
(G♭, A♭, B♭, D♭, F♭)

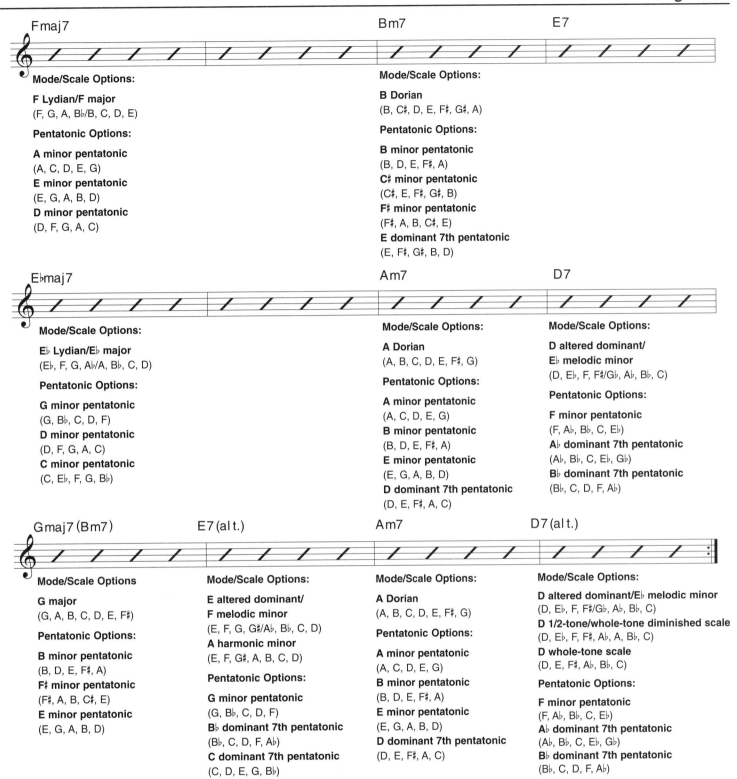

Fmaj7

Mode/Scale Options:

F Lydian/F major
(F, G, A, B♭/B, C, D, E)

Pentatonic Options:

A minor pentatonic
(A, C, D, E, G)
E minor pentatonic
(E, G, A, B, D)
D minor pentatonic
(D, F, G, A, C)

Bm7

Mode/Scale Options:

B Dorian
(B, C♯, D, E, F♯, G♯, A)

Pentatonic Options:

B minor pentatonic
(B, D, E, F♯, A)
C♯ minor pentatonic
(C♯, E, F♯, G♯, B)
F♯ minor pentatonic
(F♯, A, B, C♯, E)
E dominant 7th pentatonic
(E, F♯, G♯, B, D)

E7

E♭maj7

Mode/Scale Options:

E♭ Lydian/E♭ major
(E♭, F, G, A♭/A, B♭, C, D)

Pentatonic Options:

G minor pentatonic
(G, B♭, C, D, F)
D minor pentatonic
(D, F, G, A, C)
C minor pentatonic
(C, E♭, F, G, B♭)

Am7

Mode/Scale Options:

A Dorian
(A, B, C, D, E, F♯, G)

Pentatonic Options:

A minor pentatonic
(A, C, D, E, G)
B minor pentatonic
(B, D, E, F♯, A)
E minor pentatonic
(E, G, A, B, D)
D dominant 7th pentatonic
(D, E, F♯, A, C)

D7

Mode/Scale Options:

D altered dominant/
E♭ melodic minor
(D, E♭, F, F♯/G♭, A♭, B♭, C)

Pentatonic Options:

F minor pentatonic
(F, A♭, B♭, C, E♭)
A♭ dominant 7th pentatonic
(A♭, B♭, C, E♭, G♭)
B♭ dominant 7th pentatonic
(B♭, C, D, F, A♭)

Gmaj7 (Bm7)

Mode/Scale Options

G major
(G, A, B, C, D, E, F♯)

Pentatonic Options:

B minor pentatonic
(B, D, E, F♯, A)
F♯ minor pentatonic
(F♯, A, B, C♯, E)
E minor pentatonic
(E, G, A, B, D)

E7 (alt.)

Mode/Scale Options:

E altered dominant/
F melodic minor
(E, F, G, G♯/A♭, B♭, C, D)
A harmonic minor
(E, F, G♯, A, B, C, D)

Pentatonic Options:

G minor pentatonic
(G, B♭, C, D, F)
B♭ dominant 7th pentatonic
(B♭, C, D, F, A♭)
C dominant 7th pentatonic
(C, D, E, G, B♭)

Am7

Mode/Scale Options:

A Dorian
(A, B, C, D, E, F♯, G)

Pentatonic Options:

A minor pentatonic
(A, C, D, E, G)
B minor pentatonic
(B, D, E, F♯, A)
E minor pentatonic
(E, G, A, B, D)
D dominant 7th pentatonic
(D, E, F♯, A, C)

D7 (alt.)

Mode/Scale Options:

D altered dominant/E♭ melodic minor
(D, E♭, F, F♯/G♭, A♭, B♭, C)
D 1/2-tone/whole-tone diminished scale
(D, E♭, F, F♯, A♭, A, B♭, C)
D whole-tone scale
(D, E, F♯, A♭, B♭, C)

Pentatonic Options:

F minor pentatonic
(F, A♭, B♭, C, E♭)
A♭ dominant 7th pentatonic
(A♭, B♭, C, E♭, G♭)
B♭ dominant 7th pentatonic
(B♭, C, D, F, A♭)

OFF THE PATH

This is our last "standard," and it is another simple 16-bar chord progression that is easy to learn yet offers slightly different challenges. This time we're fundamentally in the key of F major. What I like about this tune is that in the first four bars you have a lot more time to explore the linear sounds over a major 7th chord on which you can employ either the Lydian mode or the major scale (Ionian mode). **Bars 5–8** give you another shot at the I-VI7-iim7-V7, progression and you can never practice enough over this progression. Then you are given an extended time to play over A♭ Dorian, **bars 9–12,** before returning to a cadence in F major, which becomes a quicker and more compressed turnaround accomplished in **bars 15–16**—as opposed to what you negotiated in **bars 5–8.** It's a great challenge to have all of this within one compact tune.

USING THE CD: To listen to my performed improvisation over these changes, play **Track**
33. When you're ready to do some improvising, use **Track 34.**

Example 32: Off the Path

Fmaj7

Mode/Scale Options:

F Lydian/F major
(F, G, A, B♭/B, C, D, E)

Pentatonic Options:

A minor pentatonic
(A, C, D, E, G)
E minor pentatonic
(E, G, A, B, D)
D minor pentatonic
(D, F, G, A, C)

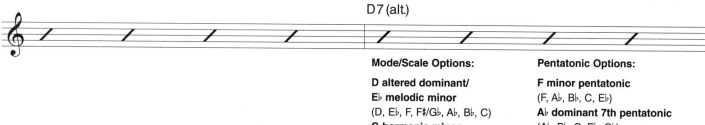

D7 (alt.)

Mode/Scale Options:

D altered dominant/
E♭ melodic minor
(D, E♭, F, F♯/G♭, A♭, B♭, C)
G harmonic minor
(D, E♭, F♯, G, A, B♭, C)

Pentatonic Options:

F minor pentatonic
(F, A♭, B♭, C, E♭)
A♭ dominant 7th pentatonic
(A♭, B♭, C, E♭, G♭)
B♭ dominant 7th pentatonic
(B♭, C, D, F, A♭)

Gm7   C7

Mode/Scale Options:

G Dorian
(G, A, B♭, C, D, E, F)

Pentatonic Options:

G minor pentatonic
(G, B♭, C, D, F)
A minor pentatonic
(A, C, D, E, G)
D minor pentatonic
(D, F, G, A, C)
C dominant 7th pentatonic
(C, D, E, G, B♭)

Steve Khan

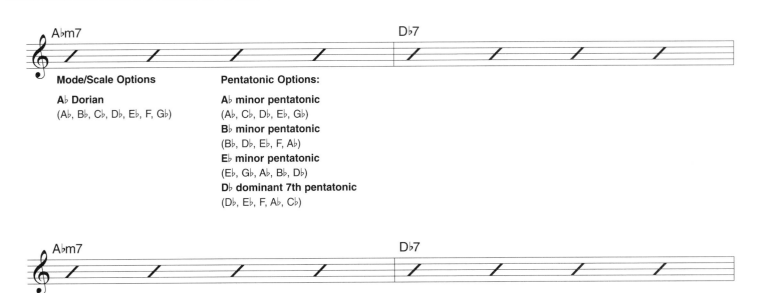

A♭m7

Mode/Scale Options

A♭ Dorian
(A♭, B♭, C♭, D♭, E♭, F, G♭)

Pentatonic Options:

A♭ minor pentatonic
(A♭, C♭, D♭, E♭, G♭)

B♭ minor pentatonic
(B♭, D♭, E♭, F, A♭)

E♭ minor pentatonic
(E♭, G♭, A♭, B♭, D♭)

D♭ dominant 7th pentatonic
(D♭, E♭, F, A♭, C♭)

D♭7

A♭m7

D♭7

Gm7

Mode/Scale Options

G Dorian
(G, A, B♭, C, D, E, F)

Pentatonic Options:

G minor pentatonic
(G, B♭, C, D, F)

A minor pentatonic
(A, C, D, E, G)

D minor pentatonic
(D, F, G, A, C)

C dominant 7th pentatonic
(C, D, E, G, B♭)

C7 (alt.)

Mode/Scale Options:

C altered dominant/
D♭ melodic minor
(C, D♭, E♭, E/F♭, G♭, A♭, B♭)

C half-tone/whole-tone
diminished scale
(C, D♭, E♭, E, F♯, G, A, B♭)

C whole-tone scale
(C, D, E, F♯, A♭, B♭)

Pentatonic Options:

E♭ minor pentatonic
(E♭, G♭ A♭, B♭, D♭)

G♭ dominant 7th pentatonic
(G♭ A♭, B♭, D♭, F♭)

A♭ dominant 7th pentatonic
(A♭, B♭, C, E♭, G♭)

Fmaj7

Mode/Scale Options:

F major
(F, G, A, B♭, C, D, E)

Pentatonic Options:

A minor pentatonic
(A, C, D, E, G)

D minor pentatonic
(D, F, G, A, C)

D7 (alt.)

Mode/Scale Options:

D altered dominant/
E♭ melodic minor
(D, E♭, F, F♯/G♭, A♭, B♭, C)

G harmonic minor
(D, E♭, F♯, G, A, B♭, C)

Pentatonic Options:

F minor pentatonic
(F, A♭, B♭, C, E♭)

A♭ dominant 7th pentatonic
(A♭, B♭, C, E♭, G♭)

B♭ dominant 7th pentatonic
(B♭, C, D, F, A♭)

Gm7

Mode/Scale Options

G Dorian
(G, A, B♭, C, D, E, F)

Pentatonic Options:

G minor pentatonic
(G, B♭, C, D, F)

A minor pentatonic
(A, C, D, E, G)

D minor pentatonic
(D, F, G, A, C)

C dominant 7th pentatonic
(C, D, E, G, B♭)

C7 (alt.)

Mode/Scale Options:

C altered dominant/
D♭ melodic minor
(C, D♭, E♭, E/F♭, G♭, A♭, B♭)

C half-tone/whole-tone
diminished scale
(C, D♭, E♭, E, F♯, G, A, B♭)

C whole-tone scale
(C, D, E, F♯, A♭, B♭)

Pentatonic Options:

E♭ minor pentatonic
(E♭, G♭, A♭, B♭, D♭)

G♭ dominant 7th pentatonic
(G♭ A♭, B♭, D♭, F♭)

A♭ dominant 7th pentatonic
(A♭, B♭, C, E♭, G♭)

Steve Khan Discography

TIGHTROPE Columbia JC 34857 1977
Sony SRCS 9386 [Japan] 1998

THE BLUE MAN Columbia JC 35539 1978
Sony SRCS 9387 [Japan] 1998

ARROWS Columbia JC 36129 1979
Sony SRCS 9545 [Japan] 1999

THE BEST OF STEVE KHAN Columbia JC 36406 1980

THE COLLECTION Columbia CK 57907 1994

Recordings featuring Randy Brecker, Michael Brecker, David Sanborn, Don Grolnick, Will Lee, Steve Gadd, Mike Mainieri, and others.

ALIVEMUTHAFORYA Columbia JC 35349 1978

Live recording featuring Steve with fellow CBS All-Stars Billy Cobham, Alphonso Johnson, Tom Scott, and a very young Mark Soskin (keyboards).

EVIDENCE Arista/Novus AN/3023 1981
RCA/Novus 3074-2-N 1990
Polydor POCJ-1892 [Japan] 1991

Solo acoustic guitar recording.

EYEWITNESS Antilles 422-848-821 1981

Polydor POCJ-1893 [Japan]

BLADES Passport Jazz PJ 88001 1982
MODERN TIMES Polydor POCJ-1894 [Japan]
CASA LOCO Antilles 422-848-822 1983
Polydor POCJ-1895 [Japan]

Steve Khan and Eyewitness recordings featuring Anthony Jackson, Steve Jordan, and Manolo Badrena.

HELPING HAND Polydor POCJ-1896 [Japan] 1987

Essentially a "best of" recording featuring selections from EYEWITNESS, MODERN TIMES, CASA LOCO, and EVIDENCE plus three new tracks featuring Clifford Carter, Bill Evans, Café, Neil Jason, and Chris Parker.

LOCAL COLOR Denon 33CY-1840 1987

Duo recording with Rob Mounsey on keyboards and Steve only on acoustic guitars.

PUBLIC ACCESS GRP GRD-9599 1989
Polydor JOOJ-20364 [Japan]

Steve Khan and Eyewitness recording featuring Anthony Jackson, Dave Weckl, and Manolo Badrena.

LET'S CALL THIS Polydor POCJ-1060 [Japan] 1991
Bluemoon R2 79163

Trio recording with Ron Carter (acoustic bass) and Al Foster (drums).

HEADLINE Polydor POCJ-1115 [Japan] 1992
Bluemoon R2 79179

Trio with Ron Carter and Al Foster. Plus three tracks with Eyewitness featuring Anthony Jackson, Dennis Chambers, and Manolo Badrena.

CROSSINGS Verve POCJ-1217 [Japan] 1994
Verve Forecast 314 523 269-2

Steve Khan and Eyewitness recording featuring Anthony Jackson, Dennis Chambers, Manolo Badrena, and Michael Brecker.

GOT MY MENTAL   Dan Contemporary TKCB-71108 [Japan]   1997
Evidence ECD 22197-2

Featuring John Patitucci (acoustic bass), Jack DeJohnette (drums), and Bobby Allende, Marc Quiñones, Don Alias, and Café on various percussion.

YOU ARE HERE   SIAM SMD-50004   1998

Duo recording with Rob Mounsey on keyboards and special guest Marc Quiñones on Latin percussion where Steve is only featured on acoustic guitar.

NEW HORIZONS   Concord Picante CCD-4878-2   2000

Caribbean Jazz Project recording featuring Steve alongside co-leaders Dave Samuels (vibes and marimba) and Dave Valentin (flute).

PARAÍSO   Concord Picante CCD-4946-2   2001

Second recording by the Caribbean Jazz Project featureing Khan, Samuels, and Valentin.

SPECIAL PROJECTS

THAT'S THE WAY I FEEL NOW - A Tribute to Thelonious Monk
    A&M Records CD 6600   1984

Track: **"Reflections,"** a duet with Steely Dan's Donald Fagen featuring Steve on acoustic guitar.

COME TOGETHER - Guitar Tribute to the Beatles
    NYC Records NYC 6004-2   1993

Track: **"Within You Without You/Blue Jay Way,"** which features Steve with Marc Johnson, Peter Erskine, and Nana Vasconcelos.

JAZZ TO THE WORLD   Blue Note CDP 7243 8 32127-2 1995

Track: **"The Christmas Waltz,"** which features the Brecker Bros. and Steve Khan.

WOULDN'T IT BE NICE - A Tribute to Brian Wilson
    Blue Note CDP 7243 8 33092-2 1997

Track: **"Don't Worry Baby (No Te Preocupes Nena),"** which features Steve with Rob Mounsey, Rubén Rodríguez, Marc Quiñones, Papo Pepin, and Gabriela Anders.

PUBLICATIONS

THE WES MONTGOMERY GUITAR FOLIO   Gopam-Enterprises

PAT MARTINO GUITAR SOLOS: The Early Years   Warner Bros. Publications

STEVE KHAN and EYEWITNESS SONGBOOK/ GUITAR WORKSHOP SERIES   Warner Bros.Publications

CONTEMPORARY CHORD KHANCEPTS   Warner Bros. Publications

AS A PRODUCER

TWO FOR THE ROAD	Larry Coryell/	Arista AB 4156	1977
	Steve Khan	BMG B19D-47025	1988
STEP IT	Bill Connors	Evidence ECD 22080-2	1985
INFERNO	Bireli Lagrene	Blue Note CDP-7-48016-2	1987
FOREIGN AFFAIRS	Bireli Lagrene	Blue Note CDP-7-90967-2	1988
TIME IN PLACE	Mike Stern	Atlantic 7-81840-2	1988
JIGSAW	Mike Stern	Atlantic 7-82027-2	1989
FANTASIA	Eliane Elias	Blue Note CDP-7-96146-2	1992
PAULISTANA	Eliane Elias	Blue Note CDP-7-89544-2	1993

Eyewitness recording *Modern Times* live at the Pit Inn, Tokyo, Japan in '82. Steve with Anthony Jackson and Manolo Badrena.

BIOGRAPHY

A special issue of Japan's *Jazz Life* magazine featured the 22 All-Time Greatest Jazz Guitarists. Of course, legends like Charlie Christian, Django Reinhardt, Wes Montgomery, Kenny Burrell, and Jim Hall were included alongside more recent giants George Benson, Pat Martino, Larry Coryell, and John McLaughlin. Listed amongst his contemporaries John Abercrombie, Pat Metheny, John Scofield, Mike Stern, and Bill Frisell was Steve Khan—a testament to a large body of work that now spans more than 30 years. It's hard to believe this dream began at a rather late age, with Wes Montgomery held as the model to which to aspire. Steve admits that, when he was a teenager, "I was a terrible drummer with no musical training. I had developed a love for the guitar, and when I was 19, I switched instruments. I decided I would not make the same mistakes I had made with the drums, so I studied hard in college along with taking private lessons from Ron Anthony." During these years, Khan always found himself in fast company, and from such situations he learned, developed, and survived. By the time he graduated from UCLA in 1969, he felt ready to make the move to New York City.

From this point forward, much of Steve's career is well documented. In 1974, he performed in one of the first contemporary jazz guitar duos with Larry Coryell. During this same period, he became a key member of the Brecker Brothers Band. His first recordings as a leader were a trio of well-received albums for Columbia Records titled *Tightrope* (1977), *The Blue Man* (1978), and *Arrows* (1979). These recordings featured Michael and Randy Brecker, David Sanborn, Don Grolnick, Will Lee, Steve Gadd, Mike Mainieri, and others. In 1994, Sony Music/Columbia released a CD compilation drawn from these three LPs titled *The Collection*.

In 1980, Steve recorded a brilliant solo acoustic guitar album, *Evidence,* which paid tribute to his earliest jazz inspirations and served to establish him as one of the great interpreters of the music of Thelonious Monk. Between 1981 and 1985, he worked and recorded steadily with his quartet, Eyewitness, which included Anthony Jackson, Manolo Badrena, and Steve Jordan. Together they made three recordings: *Eyewitness* (1981), *Modern Times/Blades* (1982), and *Casa Loco* (1983). During 1984, Steve joined Steely Dan's Donald Fagen to interpret Thelonious Monk's "Reflections" for the *That's the Way I Feel Now* recording, which was a tribute to Monk and his compositions. When Eyewitness needed a break, Khan joined Joe Zawinul's Weather Update for its one and only tour in 1986. This was followed by an innovative duet recording with keyboardist Rob Mounsey. The Grammy-nominated CD was titled *Local Color* and was released in 1987. In 1989, Eyewitness was resurrected, with Dave Weckl replacing Steve Jordan for the *Public Access* (1990) CD. Since that time, Steve has added two groundbreaking straight-ahead jazz recordings featuring Ron Carter and Al Foster: *Let's Call This* and *Headline* were released in 1991 and 1992, respectively. In 1994, Steve found himself back in the company of Anthony Jackson and Manolo Badrena, adding Dennis Chambers and Michael Brecker for *Crossings,* which is dedicated to the memory of Steve's late father, lyricist Sammy Cahn.

More recently, Steve has contributed his talents to several special projects. His unique medley of two George Harrison tunes graced Mike Mainieri's NYC Records *Come Together: A Guitar Tribute to the Beatles.* Here Steve was accompanied by Marc Johnson, Peter Erskine, and Nana Vasconcelos. Special Olympics and the holiday season brought Steve together with the Brecker Brothers for a Salsa-style interpretation of his father's one Christmas song, "The Christmas Waltz," which appeared on the CD *Jazz to the World.* In 1996 Steve teamed with Argentine vocalist Gabriela Anders, Rob Mounsey, and New York Salsa All-Stars—Rubén Rodríguez, Marc Quiñones, and Papo Pepin—to contribute "Don't Worry Baby" ("No Te Preocupes Nena") to *Wouldn't It Be Nice,* a tribute to Brian Wilson.

Recorded in 1996, *Got My Mental* brought Steve together for the first time with John Patitucci on acoustic bass and Jack DeJohnette on drums. The CD once again found him using his unique playing and arranging perspectives to interpret the works of Wayne Shorter, Ornette Coleman, Lee Morgan, Eddie Harris, and standards by Rodgers & Hammerstein, as well as Steve's father with Jimmy Van Heusen. The latter is a stunningly beautiful rendering of the Sinatra classic "The Last Dance." On four of the eight tracks,

Pentatonic Khancepts

the trio is joined at times by percussionists Bobby Allende, Marc Quiñones, and Don Alias. Brazilian percussionist Café lends his special talents to Steve's romantic journey through "I Have Dreamed." The intensity and creativity brought to these sessions showed Steve's unfaltering desire to meet new challenges and explore them. These qualities prompt the frequent mentioning of his name during discussions of contemporary jazz guitar.

In 1997 Steve reunited with Rob Mounsey to record *You Are Here*. Nearly a decade had passed since the release of *Local Color*, and the duo was eager to get back at it again. As with the previous CD, when these two talented musicians get together, the music tends to defy categorization. But the new recording seemed to sit somewhere between a contemporary version of Latin jazz and World Music jazz. Also, in keeping with their previous work, Steve is again heard only on acoustic guitars, reminding us that he is one of the instrument's most unique stylists, playing melodies and solos with a touch and phrasing all his own. One brand-new dimension for *You Are Here* was the presence of Latin percussion virtuoso Marc Quiñones. Marc brought his spirit and power to signature Khan-Mounsey compositions like "Clafouti," "Platanos Maduros," and "Peanut Soup." Released in September of 1998, the recording left little doubt that Steve and Rob are blazing a trail of their own while presenting music with broad appeal.

In August of 1998, Steve toured Japan as part of Dave Samuels' "Tribute to Cal Tjader" Group. Apart from the tremendous reaction the group received, the tour was to have more far-reaching consequences since it was here that plans were made for Steve, Dave Samuels, and Dave Valentin to become the co-leaders of the re-formed Caribbean Jazz Project. After some isolated tour dates in early 1999 for the group, Steve and Dave Samuels were asked to appear on Dave Valentin's first recording for Concord Records. Upon hearing those performances, Concord president John Burk asked to sign the Caribbean Jazz Project to his label as well. As a result of these chance events, the group's first recording with the new line-up (which then included John Benitez, bass; Richie Flores, congas; and Robert Vilera, timbales) was titled *New Horizons* and released on Concord Picante during February 2000. It features three of Steve's compositions, including "Descarga Canelón," "Charanga Sí, Sí," and "Safe and Sound (Sano y Salvo)." Since its inception, the group has toured tirelessly in Europe, South and Central America, and the U.S. April of 2001 saw the release of the Caribbean Jazz Project's second CD, *Paraíso*. Like its predecessor, it featured three new compositions from Steve: "¡Cá-ni-mo!" "El Tacaño," and "Maluco." Already considered a classic in the Latin jazz genre, the recording features Rubén Rodríguez on bass, Luisito Quintero and Dafnis Prieto sharing timbal kit duties, and the brilliant Richie Flores on congas. This very popular group returned to Europe several times in 2001, as well as more touring around the U.S. In January 2002, citing creative differences, Steve left the group to pursue other interests.

Throughout his long and distinguished career, Steve has lent his talents to recordings by such diverse artists as Miles Davis, Steely Dan, James Brown, Aretha Franklin, Quincy Jones, Eddie Palmieri, Freddie Hubbard, the Brecker Brothers, Steps Ahead, and many others too numerous to list. He has also produced recordings for fellow guitarists Larry Coryell, Mike Stern, Bireli Lagrene, and Bill Connors, as well as pianist Eliane Elias. In addition, he has published four highly regarded books: *Wes Montgomery Guitar Folio; Pat Martino: The Early Years; Guitar Workshop Series: Steve Khan* (which really functions as an Eyewitness songbook); and the influential *Contemporary Chord Khancepts*. Steve has also become one of the most in-demand music clinicians and teachers while continuing to perform in clubs and concert halls throughout the U.S., Central and South America, Europe, and Japan.

Steve caught live at the Pit Inn, Tokyo, Japan in '82 while recording *Modern Times*.

The *Just Jazz Real Book* features 250 classic jazz tunes. These songs form the required core repertoire for all working jazz musicians.

THE BEST IN Jazz

The Just Real Book Series

The most complete and accurate fakebook series of all time.

Each fakebook in the *Just Real Book* series contains hundreds of songs that are the core repertoire for musicians all over the world. Original composer sources were consulted to ensure that the arrangements remained true to the composers' intention. Plus, useful and important chord substitutions are indicated for each arrangement. Each book is extensively cross-referenced with appendices including: a complete composer index, a complete discography, a section on how to play from a fakebook, chord theory reference pages, and a section on how to create interesting chord substitutions. Comb bound.

Just Standards Real Book

C Edition	(FBM0002)	$39.95
B♭ Edition	(FBM0002BF)	$39.95
E♭ Edition	(FBM0002EF)	$39.95

Just Jazz Real Book

C Edition	(FBM0003)	$39.95
B♭ Edition	(FBM0003BF)	$39.95
E♭ Edition	(FBM0003EF)	$39.95
Bass Clef Edition	(FBM0003BS)	$39.95

Just Blues Real Book

C Edition	(FBM0004)	$39.95

The 21st Century Pro Method Series

The most complete method for the modern jazz guitarist.

Jazz Guitar—Swing to Bebop

Spiral-Bound Book and CD
(0388B) $24.95
This book covers music theory, scales, modes, chord voicings, arpeggios, soloing, and comping. More than 180 music examples and 16 complete solos in the styles of many jazz greats are used to place all concepts in the context of classic jazz chord progressions and standards. A CD with all the music examples is included!

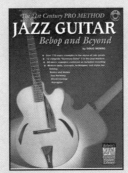

Jazz Guitar—Bebop and Beyond

Spiral-Bound Book and CD
(0609B) $24.95
This book explores advanced, modern jazz and bebop concepts, and techniques, including music theory, scales, modes, chord voicings, arpeggios, soloing, and comping concepts. More than 170 music examples and 13 complete solos in the styles of many jazz greats are used to place all concepts into a practical musical context. A CD with all the music examples is included!

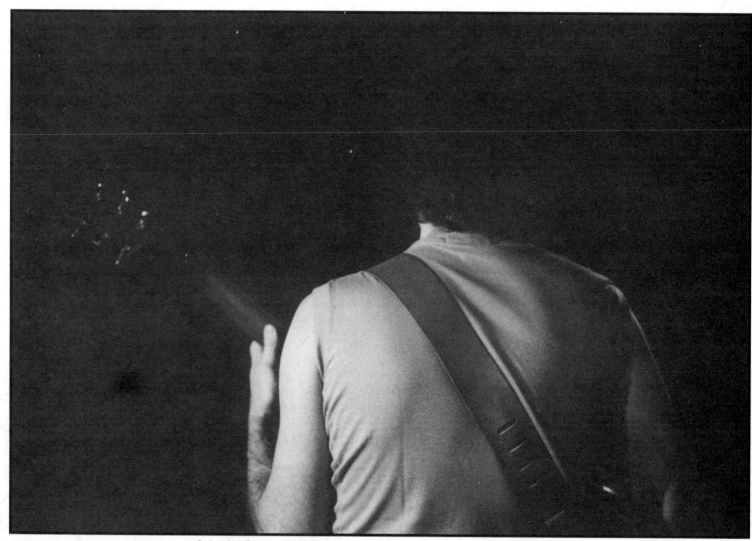

A view fron Steve's perspective as Eyewitness performs at the Pit Inn, Tokyo, Japan in '82.